THE

CANDIDATE'S

HANDBOOK

for

Winning Local Elections

By

Harvey Yorke

and

Liz Doherty

Published by Harvey Yorke, Novato, CA.

DEDICATION

To the good citizens who give their time and energy in the cause of better local government--and to the thousands of wonderful people who work tirelessly to elect their friends and neighbors to public offices.

Published by Harvey Yorke
Box 252, Novato CA   94948

Second printing March 1982

Library of Congress Catalog Card No. 81-90654

Manufactured in the United States of America

Printed by Wildwood Press, Woodacre CA

Typesetting by Word Processing Specialists, Inc., Novato CA

ISBN 0-9607598-0-8

CONTENTS

PREFACE

Local government has more impact on our daily lives than either state or federal government. We look to local agencies for police and fire protection, schools, community colleges, hospitals, water and sanitary services, land use and community planning, street repairs, parks, recreation programs and much more.

One of the great traditions in this country is that citizens are willing to take time from their families and their work to serve their communities as elected officials. We should do everything possible to encourage this form of citizen participation in government.

In a sense, The Candidate's Handbook for Winning Local Elections promotes citizen participation by taking much of the mystery out of organizing and campaigning for local, non-partisan offices. The material is presented in logical sequence, in plain language. No experience in politics is necessary to understand the campaign process.

I consider this book as "must" reading for anyone seeking election to city, county or special district offices. It is as valuable for campaign managers and volunteers as for candidates.

March Fong Eu
Secretary of State
State of California

INTRODUCTION

This book is for people with little or no political experience who want to be elected to any of the thousands of local government offices--and for their friends who want to help them as campaign managers and committee members.

In California alone there are more than 5,200 elected governing bodies at the county, city and special district levels, among them:

County Boards of Supervisors
County Boards of Education
County Superintendent of Schools
Community College Boards
Hospital District Boards
City and Town Councils
School Boards
Fire District Boards
Water District Boards
Sanitary District Boards
Lighting District Boards
Community Service District Boards

Several hundred more individual offices are filled by elected officials:

...at the county level:

District Attorney
Sheriff
County Clerk
Assessor
Auditor
Controller
Superior Court Judges

...and in some cities:

Mayor
City Attorney
City Clerk
Municipal Court Judges

Collectively, these are known in official language as local, non-partisan offices. Candidates do not represent political parties and some of the laws governing their elections differ from laws covering partisan races for state and federal offices.

This brings up the subject of the content of the book.

Election laws differ from state to state. This book is based on California laws in effect in 1981. But, because state laws and local city and county ordinances affecting campaigns change frequently, check with your City Clerk or County Clerk before you start planning a campaign.

Local election campaigns differ considerably in size, scope, cost, duration and intensity. This makes it difficult to write a candidate's handbook to cover all situations, as would be apparent if you compared races, say, for Mayor of a big city and for a suburban School District or Fire District board.

To overcome this writing problem, we assumed that most of our readers would be relatively new to the campaigning process and that their campaigns would be staffed primarily with volunteers. Thus we have gone into considerable detail on planning, preparing and campaigning. However, even seasoned campaigners will find this volume useful, particularly the detailed checklists in the Appendix.

The format is designed to give you a combination training guide and management tool.

Part I is a series of nine chapters which cover major topics in the order in which you deal with them, from making the decision to run for public office, through organizing and fundraising to campaigning and financial reporting.

Part II is a series of essays on subjects of special interest, largely "how to" discussions of campaign functions, such as Phone Banks, invitational events, handling volunteers and election day get-out-the-vote efforts. Samples of campaign materials are also included.

Part III, the Appendix, is a management tool for candidates, managers and committee members. It contains checklists to cover just about every campaign function.

The writing style is worth brief mention.

We use "you" throughout the text, usually meaning the candidate. However, it is apparent at times that we are addressing the Campaign Manager, Finance Chairman or people in charge of other aspects of the campaign.

We also employ "chairman" throughout the text, not to be sexist, but for convenience. We hope you don't mind.

To make reading easier, we violated a few rules of English composition—using dashes or parentheses to separate phrases, instead of commas, and by listing some topics and phrases in column form, instead of the customary separation by semicolons. Please don't report us for these violations.

As for campaigning in general...

We cannot emphasize too strongly--or too often--the need for organization and planning in campaigns. These two elements mean the difference between victory and defeat.

Campaigning is fun; also hard work for everyone involved. If we have made your job a little more pleasant and a little easier, we will have succeeded in our goal.

Good luck! Good campaigning!

Harvey Yorke

Liz Doherty

Novato, California

ABOUT THE AUTHORS

Harvey Yorke, a former Novato CA (pop. 40,000) City Council member, has over 35 years' experience in public relations. He is now an independent consultant and writer on public relations, communications and government affairs.

Mr. Yorke served on Governor Reagan's staff in Sacramento, as public relations director for U.S. Senator S. I. Hayakawa and as assistant to the president of Whitaker & Baxter International, a San Francisco-based public relations consulting firm.

In city and county campaigns, Mr. Yorke has served as manager, advisor and consultant for candidates and on ballot initiative measures.

A graduate of Stanford University and former Los Angeles newspaperman, Mr. Yorke is an accredited member of the Public Relations Society of America and a director of the Public Relations Round Table of San Francisco. He is a member of the Society for Technical Communications and a retired U.S. Air Force Lt. Colonel.

Liz Doherty entered politics as a teenage volunteer in San Francisco and has over 20 years' experience as an organizer, manager, consultant and volunteer.

Her experience includes City Council, Special District, District Attorney, U.S. Senate and presidential campaigns, along with city and county ballot initiative measures. She managed three successful campaigns for her husband, Joe, as a member of the Marin County Community College Board of Trustees.

Mrs. Doherty is a specialist in precinct organization, phone banks, get-out-the-vote campaigns, organizing volunteers and planning special events.

The mother of two daughters, Mrs. Doherty is active with non-profit and charitable organizations. She has been a successful fundraiser for the Musuclar Dystrophy Association in Marin County and for Vine Village, a home for retarded adults, located in Napa CA.

PART I

CHAPTER 1

WHAT
EVERY CANDIDATE
NEEDS TO KNOW

ABOUT DECIDING TO RUN FOR OFFICE...

...be sure you really want the job...make certain your family accepts the idea...examine your qualifications...estimate your name recognition factor and bases of support...talk with people who have been through the process...

ABOUT GETTING ORGANIZED...

...start early...first, prepare to answer questions about your

1

qualifications, support, views, campaign plans, costs...discuss your ideas with small groups of friends...form an Organizing Committee...find a good Campaign Manager...work methodically to build a strong team...

ABOUT PLANNING...

...you deal with major policy and strategy decisions...let your committee handle details...research issues, voting patterns, other matters...decide a campaign strategy...list campaign activities and support materials...establish a timetable...assign responsibilities...write a budget...anticipate problems...

ABOUT FUNDRAISING...

...find a strong Finance Chairman...appoint a Treasurer...organize a Finance Committee...establish a fundraising strategy...prepare lists of prospects...print pledge cards and a Candidate Fact Sheet...set a timetable...get started early...

ABOUT CAMPAIGN MATERIALS...

...list campaign materials needed...be cost-effective in selecting materials...set production priorities...use a "color theme" in your campaign...allow time for production...

ABOUT CAMPAIGNING...

...keep your eye on the target: votes...phase your campaign: expanding name recognition, support building, debating issues, appealing for votes...pace the campaign to peak just before the election...spend your time meeting voters...leave details to your Campaign Committee...

ABOUT CAMPAIGN REPORTS...

...California law requires a Treasurer and reports of all contributions and expenditures...get help from your City or County Clerk and the Fair Political Practices Commission...

ABOUT OTHER MATTERS...

...Part II of the book offers essays on topics of special interest in campaigns: organizing invitational events, polls and surveys, Phone Banks, coffees, get-out-the-vote campaigns, news tips, advertising...also in Part II are sample Statements of Qualifications, campaign budgets and a start-to-finish campaign schedule...the Appendix contains checklists for every need in planning, organizing and running a campaign.

CHAPTER 2

DECIDING TO RUN FOR OFFICE

Investigate carefully before deciding.

Not many people wake up one morning to announce: "I am a candidate for public office!"

The decision evolves over a period of time. It is usually the end of the Natural Evolution road or the Lingering Dream sequence.

Natural Evolution concerns people who become involved in community affairs, gain knowledge and recognition, then see the next natural step to be as a candidate for election. Friends speed up the process by suggesting they run for office.

The Lingering Dream affects people who harbor the idea in the backs of their minds for a long time that "someday I'd like to run for public office." Given the right circumstances, like a stable career and family situation, and they decide to make the move.

However you arrived at the point of considering running for office doesn't much matter. You face the same basic questions before you can make a final decision:

1. **Prepare to answer these questions:**

    * Do I really want to be an elected official?

    * Can I put up with the demands of politics?

    * Can my family accept the idea?

    * How will my job (or career) be affected?

2. **Is this the time to run and the right office?**

   * Is this the right time, personally and politically, to run for public office?

   * Would another time--a later election--be better?

   * Is this the office I want, considering my interests, qualifications and personal ambitions?

3. **Can I win?**

   * Do I have the name recognition?

   * Do I have the support I need--people and money--for a winning campaign?

   * What kind of opposition can I anticipate?

However you answer these questions is up to you, of course. But the decision-making job is easier if you take it in two stages:

First, deal with personal and family questions.

Second, take up the questions of timing and ability to win.

There is a lot to consider before you make up your mind. One of the best things to do is to talk with people who have been through the process--particularly people who have served in the office you are considering.

As you talk to people, focus on four topics:

   * **Time.**
   Be sure you are clear on the amount of time required for an election--and then to do the job after you are elected. Find out how much time it takes to prepare for meetings, how much time is needed for meetings and related official and social activities. Calculate what this means to your family and your work.

   * **Workload.**
   How technical is the work? Is special knowledge required, new skills?

   * **Privacy.**
   You and your family lose a degree of privacy when you become a public official. In California, you are also required to file annual personal financial disclosure reports. How will this affect you and your family?

5

* **Frustration.**
  You cannot avoid a certain amount of frustration in public life: colleagues out-voting you; the public failing to appreciate your efforts; limitations imposed by state and federal laws. How much will this bother you?

As for estimating your ability to win an election, you can only guess at this time. But you can get something of an idea by answering the types of questions you will be asked when you go out looking for help with the campaign:

* How much name recognition do you have?

* What bases of support do you have--first for money and people to campaign; later to win votes?

* What kind of opposition do you anticipate: issues, candidates, other?

* What will a campaign cost? Can you raise the money?

* Do you have any personal problems--business conflicts of interest, skeletons in the closet, other problems--which could surface to cause troubles?

After you have completed your private investigation, tally the score:

* Do you want to be a political candidate?

* Is this the office you want?

* Do you have a fair chance of winning?

Now verify some of your conclusions:

...meet with a few trusted friends. Tell them what you are thinking and ask for their frank opinions.

...talk with some of the old-timers and currently active people in local politics. See what they think about your chances. Listen carefully to their advice--very carefully.

...make some preliminary moves toward organizing. Look for one person to take on the job of chairing your Organizing Committee and several more good people to work for you.

...ask a few key people in the community what they think about your running for office. Include in this group some of the people who usually contribute to local campaigns, editors and reporters (if you know them well enough to talk in confidence) and people who have a "feel" for local politics. Note whether people greet the idea of your candidacy with great or only mild enthusiasm.

Nothing remains now but to make a decsion. If it is yes, move quickly to start organizing. If it is no, or not at this time, start planning and preparing for the time when you will be a candidate. If you have gone this far, there is no question that some day you will be a candidate for public office.

CHAPTER 3

GETTING ORGANIZED

**There is a time to quit talking and to start organizing.
That is the instant you decide to become a candidate.**

Organizing is a big job. You cannot afford to waste time, even if your election is many months away. But you can simplify the job by being methodical.

Essentially, there are two tasks involved: preparing yourself; building an organization.

The end product you want is a team to help you:

* Raise money.

* Recruit and organize volunteers.

* Gather information and plan the campaign.

* Prepare campaign materials.

* Campaign.

* Prepare and file required reports.

SELF-PREPARATION

You cannot ask people for their time or their money until you are ready to answer their questions and you have a few written materials in hand. Nor can you start organizing until you have some kind of plan in mind.

This is what you do:

1. Prepare to answer these questions:

* Why are you running?

* What do you hope to accomplish if elected?

* What are your qualifications for the job?

* How much name recognition do you have?

* What are your bases of support?

* What are the issues and your positions on them?

* What kind of campaign do you plan?

* What will it cost?

* Do you have any personal problems which might interfere, from political problems to skeletons in the closet?

* (You may also be asked about political ambitions, political philosophies, issues unrelated to the campaign and any number of personal matters.)

2. **Write a few basic materials:**

* **A personal fact sheet.**
To help people get to know you, type a one-page summary of your education, qualifications, community activities and views on major issues. (This becomes your Candidate Fact Sheet when you start raising money and recruiting committee members, until you replace it with a printed brochure.)

* **A tentative budget.**
For potential major contributors and others concerned with costs, prepare a simple budget. List estimates by major categories: printing, mailing, advertising, campaign materials, overhead (if you plan a campaign headquarters). Treat this as a confidential document; there's no sense in tipping off the opposition the kind of campaign you plan.

3. **List known and potential supporters:**

* Friends and relatives.

* People who have offered help.

* Organizations.

* Groups which share your interests and views.

* Experienced campaigners in the community.

* Money sources.

* People for specific campaign positions.

* People with special skills.

* Help from outside the area.

4. **Plan your organizing moves:**
With the help of a few friends, make a simple plan and timetable for getting organized:

* Individuals to contact to take committee jobs.

* In what order you will contact people.

* How you will approach people: individually, in small groups, through intermediaries.

* Starting and completion dates for organizing chores.

    Example: (For June '82 Board of Supervisors primary):
    Sept. 1, 1981   Start assembling support lists.
    Sept. 5   - Treasurer and temporary Organizing Committee Chairman selected.
    Sept. 9   - Organizing Committee formed.
    Sept. 15 - Support lists completed.
    Sept. 15 - Start writing preliminary fundraising plan.
    Sept. 18 - Order pledge cards (for fundraising).
    Sept. 20 - Start planning candidacy announcement for late Oct. or early Nov.
    Oct. 1   - Target date to have Campaign Manager and Campaign committee in place.

5. **Set up files and a checklist:**
Don't rely on memory. Establish a simple filing system, even if it is only a notebook. Keep a running checklist so you can mark off chores as they are completed and add new ones as the organizing progresses. (See checklists #1, #2, and #3 in Appendix.)

BUILDING A CAMPAIGN ORGANIZATION

When building a campaign organization, keep your eye on the end product, a smooth-working team to give you help with specific functions: planning...fundraising...preparing campaign materials...building support...reaching voters.

Naturally, the size of the organization and some of the functions depend upon the type of race. In a countywide race, for example, you will probably need a campaign headquarters and, perhaps, district or area committees. Conversely , in a low-key, non-controversial race for district seat, a small all-purpose committee is satisfactory.

But remember, regardless of the type of political contest, the basic campaign functions must be handled: planning, fundraising, production of materials, support-building and reaching the voters.

This is one way to proceed:

Step 1 - Start with small group meetings.

Arrange to meet with small groups of people--10 at most--to discuss your ideas and listen to their advice.

Begin with people you know well: family, friends, close associates, people who have expressed interest in your candidacy.

Give out your personal fact sheet. Discuss the questions we listed earlier in this chapter. Spot people you would like to have either on your Campaign Committee, as part of an advisory group, or on the Organizing Committee.

Repeat this process with several groups, until you have spotted enough people to form an Organizing Committee.

Step 2 - Form an Organizing Committee.

This is an informal group, organized for the sole purpose of helping you make some basic policy decisions and to recruit people for key positions in your Campaign Committee.

Make this distinction clear when you ask people to be part of the group. This relieves the fears that some people have of becoming more involved than they wish to be.

Step 3 - Find a Campaign Manager.

The single most important person on your team is the Campaign Manager. It does not matter what title you use--Chairman, Coordinator, Manager, or something else--you need someone to take charge of the organization and the campaign.

There is a saying in the legal profession: "A lawyer who defends himself has a fool for a client." The same is true in politics: "A candidate who runs his own campaign has a fool for a candidate."

Your manager does not have to be an expert in politics--just good at organizing and managing people. He or she must also be someone you trust and whose advice you value.

You may want to have one person serve as Campaign Committee Chairman and another as Campaign Manager. This is particularly

11

useful when you can find a prominent person to accept the "Chairman" title to attract supporters, with the understanding that he or she will not be saddled with the management chores.

If you are fortunate, you may find a Campaign Manager before you start the series of small group meetings. Otherwise, you have to make a separate search for this person, or pick someone within the Organizing Committee.

Step 4 - Put the Organizing Committee to work.

Ask one person to chair the Organizing Committee. This relieves you of the work of planning and running meetings.

Next, give the committee its marching orders:

1. To help you with some basic decisions about organization, operating policies and strategies.

2. To find people for key committee positions: Campaign Manager, Treasurer, Finance Chairman and Precinct Chairman or Volunteer Coordinator.

3. To begin organizing the fundraising effort: assembling lists, preparing materials (fact sheets, pledge cards), forming the nucleus of a fundraising committee and, perhaps, starting to make contacts for money and pledges.

4. To start assembling information for use in planning the campaign (the beginning of the research activity): filing dates and fees; printing and advertising costs; postal regulations and fees; voting patterns in recent elections; information on issues and potential opposition candidates.

5. To establish a schedule and a timetable for completing the organizing task. Have them list the order in which things will be done, who is responsible for each action and starting and ending dates for tasks.

Step 5 - Decide the campaign structure.

You and the Organizing Committee need to decide two things at this point:

...the size and type of campaign organization.

...how it will be managed.

Size and type of organization depend upon the type of race you are in, the area you must cover, how intense the campaign will be and the number of campaign workers you estimate will be available. You can get some help with this decision by reviewing Checklist #3 in the Appendix which lists and defines committee positions.

As for management, the most effective system in local campaigns is the Campaign Manager to run the show with the help of a Steering Committee to advise him and the candidate. The Steering Committee is chaired by the Campaign Manager and includes the Finance Chairman, Treasurer and Precinct Chairman, plus a few more people chosen for their knowledge of campaigning and the community.

Step 6 - Decide on paid help.

Even in very small campaigns, the question of paid help often arises simply because there are not enough volunteers for some of the critical work.

It used to be that campaigns were run entirely by volunteers, especially local campaigns. But times have changed. Many of the people who volunteered in the past have gone back to work, part-time or full-time. Second, some of the former volunteers who became experts at various tasks now want to be paid for their work.

Your decision--you and the Organizing Committee--depends, again, on the type of campaign, but here are the areas to consider:

* **A campaign management firm.**
  This is expensive--usually for high-budget, big city races.

* **Consultants.**
  Paid consultants can be used for planning, news media work, developing strategies, advising the Campaign Manager and reviewing progress.

* **A paid manager.**
  In some campaigns it is worth the cost of a paid manager--professional or semi-professional--with a good track record in your kind of campaign. The person could be paid a nominal fee for the early stages and more money for full-time work the last several weeks.

* **A paid office manager.**
  This is a virtual necessity when you have a campaign headquarters operating daily. A local person with experience in the work is satisfactory.

Step 7 - Decide financial policies.

Handling money in a political campaign can be a headache--or worse. One way to avoid problems is with a simple set of policies, like these:

1. **Separate the money-handling functions:**

   * The Finance Chairman and committee members raise money but do not spend it.

   * The Treasurer is limited to banking money and paying bills after they are approved by the Campaign Manager, plus providing financial reports and filing reports with the (California) Fair Political Practices Commission (FPPC).

   * Only the Campaign Manager authorizes expenditures, and those according to the budget. However, he should make provisions for the Office Manager and others to spend minor amounts for necessities.

   * Chairmen of working committees (publicity, advertising, events, etc.) can incur bills for specific purposes, according to their budgets.

   * A Budget Committee, when used, only allocates funds among functions. It cannot approve spending.

   * The candidate is out of the money picture, except to solicit contributions and to receive checks which are given immediately to the Treasurer for banking.

2. **Establish a two-signature bank account.**

   Require two signatures on all checks--usually the Treasurer and one other person--but have three signatures on file at the bank so two people are always available.

3. **Limit cash transactions.**

   * Check FPPC regulations. Contributions to political campaigns must be by check or "in-kind" services (such as printing). The only time cash can be accepted is at fundraising events. Even then there are restrictions.

   * Pay all bills by check, except for a limited petty cash fund for incidentals, these requiring receipts.

4.   Require bids for services.

Require bids--get several if possible--for services such as printing, sign painting, equipment rental, etc.   Prices for some goods and services vary widely, even in small communities.

5.   Decline certain contributions.

List individuals and organizations whose contributions are undesired or unacceptable, such as people who expect favors or other special consideration in return for their contributions.

6.   Depositing contributions.

Have fundraisers give all contributions to the Treasurer the day they are received, if possible; the following day at the latest. This avoids lost contributions.   Then have all contributions deposited in the bank so records are accurate.   Bookkeeping problems can result if contribution checks are endorsed to another person to pay bills.

7.   Loans.

Non-interest-bearing loans can be made to the campaign committee by any person, including the candidate.   These will be handled according to FPPC regulations, including repayment or forgiveness (non-repayment).   Bank or other interest-bearing loans must have advance approval of the candidate and the Steering Committee.

8.   Financial statements.

The Treasurer must provide weekly financial statements to the candidate, Campaign Manager and Steering Committee: total received and spent; amount committed but not yet spent.

Step 8 - Form the Campaign Committee; assign responsibilities.

When people are available for the major Campaign Committee positions--Chairman, Manager, Finance Chairman, Treasurer, Precinct Chairman, Steering Committee--dissolve the Organizing Committee and form the official Campaign Committee.

Assign all members of the Organizing Committee to specific jobs in the campaign.   Don't make the mistake of leaving anyone without a job who wants to work in the campaign.

At this point, every campaign function should be covered, either as part of a committee or as a separate committee.   Someone is designated to be responsible for each activity, reporting to the Campaign Manager.

Your role as candidate now changes. You have a team behind you to provide support and assistance. From here on, let the Campaign Committee run your life--tell you where to go, when, what to do and say.

You still have a voice in campaign affairs, but be willing to limit yourself to major policy decisions. Trust your committee to steer you on the right course. But at the same time, demand performance. If things are not going well, take up the problems with the Campaign Manager and the Steering Committee.

Now you're organized. Get out and start campaigning!

CHAPTER 4

PLANNING

Good planning pays off in votes.

Planning is the simple process of setting goals and deciding how to reach them. We do it every day in our personal and professional lives.

Planning is an inherent part of the campaigning process, from deciding what kind of organization to form, to organizing fund-raising and other campaign events.

What is the payoff? Plenty:

...better use of resources: time, money, people.

...clear goals.

...early identification of problems.

...ability to avoid pitfalls.

...everyone "marching in the same direction."

To help you and your committee with the planning task, this chapter deals with the subject in two ways:

* First, we discuss the seven basic elements which are involved in any plan.

* Second, we apply these elements, providing an outline for writing your own campaign plan.

BASIC ELEMENTS IN PLANNING

Seven basic elements are involved in any situation:

1. Goals.
A definition of specific objectives.

2. Research.
Assemble facts: identify problems; pinpoint strengths and weaknesses; identify allies and opposition; study issues; analyze your data.

3. Strategies.
Select courses of action; decide policies.

4. Support.
List the materials and people you need.

5. Schedule.
Establish a timetable for starting and completing every action; establish priorities.

6. Responsibilities.
Assign responsibility for each decision and action.

7. Budget.
Put a price tag on every item and action.

HOW TO WRITE A CAMPAIGN PLAN

Some campaign plans can be written on a single sheet of paper, including the budget. Others can be as big as a telephone book. The size of your plan will depend upon the type of election and how much detail you want to include.

The following is what you would include in a hotly-contested race for a countywide office (Sheriff, District Attorney, Assessor, Controller, County Clerk), a county Board of Supervisors seat, or a large city election for Mayor or City Council. The assumption is that you have the time and money to plan and campaign properly.

1.   **Goals.**
      The ultimate goal is to win the election, of course. But in writing the campaign plan you might want to identify other goals which tie into strategies, such as "Freeze out other candidates," or "Win in the primary."

2.   **Research.**

      * **Assemble facts:** Filing dates and fees; postal regulations and mailing costs; sign ordinances; printing other production costs; sources of services; advertising rates and a list of publications.

      * **Voting patterns:** Check County Clerk records of recent elections to identify precincts with high and low voter turnout; list precincts by turnout rate; try to identify voting patterns for age, occupations, interest and ethnic groups.

      * **Voter attitudes:** Determine, with a poll or other means, what attitudes prevail among voters which might affect the election, such as high or low confidence in local government.

      * **Issues:** Major issues are apparent. But many voters respond to localized or neighborhood issues, such as crime problems, park needs, zoning questions, street repairs; identify these localized issues by area. Also identify any subjects which might become campaign issues later.

      * **External influences:** What external issues might affect the campaign, such as a controversial statewide measure on the ballot? List all possibilities and analyze them.

      * **Strengths and weaknesses:** What are the candidate's greatest strengths and apparent weaknesses? What can be done to improve his or her position?

      * **Allies and opposition:** List known and potential allies (individuals and groups); do the same for known and potential opposition in the area.

      * **Name Identification:** Estimate the candidate's name recognition factor in the voting area, using a survey or other means. Determine how it can be improved. (The essay on Building Name Recognition and Checklist #7 will help.)

3. Strategies.

Strategies are simple statements of what you intend to do in a variety of situations. These are examples:

* Declare early to discourage other candidates and to corner sources of money.

* Wait until late to declare, when issues are clear.

* Make a strong effort to win in the primary; try to avoid having to run a second campaign for the general election.

* Concentrate on pockets of known support.

* Rely on grass roots, precinct organizing, with emphasis on door-to-door campaigning.

* Organize by districts with mini-committees and among business, professional, interest and ethnic groups, each with its own leadership.

* Issues: campaign on a single issue; on major issues only; on neighborhood issues.

* Campaign for change in local government policies.

* Opponents: ignore them and run as the best qualified person; attack opponents; attack only incumbents; capitalize on their campaign mistakes.

* Coattail on a state or national candidate.

4. Support.

* Materials: List campaign materials to be used. (Refer to Chapter 6 and Checklist #11.)

* Organization: List committees and functions. (Refer to Checklist #3.)

* List organizations which have offered to conduct campaigns among their members on your behalf.

5. Schedule.

* List all activities planned for the campaign in sequence, beginning with the earliest date.

* Also make a production timetable: starting and completion dates for each item produced and each event planned; list names of people responsible for every step.

6.   Responsibility.
Make a person or committee responsible for every decision and action in the campaign.   This can be done in two formats: either list names of responsible people in the body of the plan, as part of a schedule or list of activities, or publish the list of responsibilities as an appendix to the plan.

7.   Budget.
Treat the campaign budget as a confidential document to avoid giving opponents an unearned advantage.   One way is to limit distribution to members of the Steering Committee.

Budgets can be written in two ways: an outline, or General Budget; every item listed, a Detailed Budget.   Samples of both are in Part II of the book.

CHAPTER 5

FUNDRAISING

You need money to communicate with voters.

You don't want to finance your own campaign. Even if you can afford it, it's not smart. If you can't get people to contribute money to get you elected, there is a question whether you have the support you need to win the election.

Solution: Organize a fundraising campaign--early!

Basically, what you need for fundraising is:

* A strong Finance Chairman and an active committee.

* A Treasurer to bank money and keep records.

* Lists of prospective contributors.

* Support materials (pledge cards, fact sheets).

* A plan of action.

* Understanding of fundraising techniques.

You should also be aware that...

...everything is cash and carry in political campaigns.

...you don't need all the money at the beginning of the campaign; only enough to get started.

HOW TO ORGANIZE AND PREPARE

1.   Find a strong Finance Chairman.
Put fundraising in the hands of a strong Finance Chairman who...

...knows <u>where</u> to find money.

...knows <u>how</u> to get it.

...is persistent, self-motivated, well-organized.

...is committed to help you win the election.

Help the chairman form a committee, then step back and let the committee do the job.

2.   Assemble and annotate lists.
Help the committee to assemble lists of all possible sources of money, including:

* Friends and relatives--yours; committee members.

* Known and possible supporters.

* Contributors in previous local elections.

* Anyone affected by the outcome of the election.

* People who share your interests and views.

* PACs--business/union Political Action Committees.

* Friends outside your voting area.

Annotate the lists.   For each name, indicate:

* How much to ask for.

* People who can "open doors" to money.

* Habitual contributors.

* Who makes group decisions--or influences them.

* Anything else which might help raise money.

3.   Write a simple plan of action.

* Amount needed for the entire campaign.

* Dates when specific amounts are needed.
* A list of fundraising events.
* A calendar or timetable for action.
* List of materials needed: Pledge cards, fact sheets, flyers, invitations to fundraising events, postage.
* A fundraising budget.

Also build in safeguards...

...procedures for handling contributions according to FPPC regulations--including in-kind services.

...guidelines for rejecting contributions, such as those from individuals or groups expecting favors or special treatment if you are elected.

...procedures for handling bad checks.

...policies for "forgiving" (not repaying) all or part of personal loans to the Campaign Committee in the event the fundraising fails to raise enough money.

4. Prepare materials.

* Pledge cards.
To save money, combine them with Endorsement/Volunteer cards (sample in Part II.)

While waiting for delivery of the printed cards, use a typewritten substitute--printed quickly and inexpensively by any "instant" print shop; two on each 8½x11" sheet to reduce costs.

Print plenty of cards--at least enough for 30% of the registered voters. Remember, the cost per card goes down as the volume ordered goes up.

* Candidate fact sheet.
This is an interim item, for use until your brochure is printed. The fact sheet you prepared before organizing the Campaign Committee is satisfactory.

* A campaign budget and spending schedule.
This is for internal use. However, some major contributors may want information to determine the size and amount of their contributions. Treat this information as confidential; you don't want to tip off the opposition to your plans.

* Financial records.

The Treasurer needs a record-keeping system to comply with FPPC regulations.

WHO CONTRIBUTES--AND WHY

Who contributes:

* Families and friends of candidates and committee members.

* Committee members.

* Business/Professional/Union: individuals, their associations, PACs (Political Action Committees).

* Members of organizations friendly to the candidate.

* Groups interested in election results.

* "Habitual" campaign contributors.

* People "turned on" by the candidate.

Why individuals and groups contribute:

* Friendship: candidate or fundraiser.

* Issues.

* Interests in common with the candidate.

* To change/not change the government agency.

* The candidate's charm or other qualities.

* Friends/neighbors contributed.

* Excitement generated at an event.

* 1001 unknown reasons.

FUNDRASING HINTS

* Say thanks--make a friend.

* Acknowledge contributions in writing, immediately--signed by the candidate.

* People don't give unless asked--so ask!

* When people play "follow the leader"--waiting to see who

else contributes--go after leaders first.

* Use intermediaries with some people.

* You can't "come back to the well" for second contributions; ask for enough the first time.

* If you ask for too much, you may be turned down.

* If you ask for too little, you lose money.

* Estimate what individuals and organizations might be willing to give--and ask for that amount.

* Give people the option of signing pledge cards.

* Follow up on unpaid pledges.

* Reject contributions from anyone--individual or group--who expects something in return after the election.

* At fundraisers, have several people primed to make contributions early; this stimulates others to give.

* Make giving easy at events: place bowls, jars, boxes and other receptacles in prominent places.

* Use sign-in sheets at events to get names.

TECHNIQUES THAT WORK

1. Pledge cards.
Distribute the cards as widely as possible. Most are signed during events, like receptions, coffees and kickoff parties. Be sure the Finance Committee follows through to collect the money pledged.

2. Receptions.
Ask people to host receptions in their homes, inviting friends, neighbors and associates--anounced in advance as fundraising events. A Finance Committee member makes the pitch for money; the candidate talks about campaign issues.

3. Receptions with guest hosts.
Look for sponsors who will pay the cost of a fundraising reception. Sometimes the host invites guests; sometimes your committee provides the list or invites people.

4. Fundraising events.

Let your imagination go.   Plan events that work in your community:

...picnics...ball games...spaghetti feeds...chicken roasts.

...theater parties...swimming meets...luncheons...dinners.

...anything which gives participants a good time in return for their contributions.

5. The peer approach.

Have prospective contributors approached by people they consider as their social or professional equals--especially among major contributors.

6. Organization/Association contributions.

Some organizations have fixed procedures for interviewing and investigating before making contributions to political campaigns. Learn the rules for each group.

Be prepared to answer questions, perhaps for an hour in some instances.   Answer clearly and truthfully.

Discuss issues and topics of known interest to each group.

7. In-kind contributions.

Some business, professional and union organizations perfer to give services or to provide equipment instead of contributing money. These are called "in-kind" contributions--as good as cash--also reportable under FPPC rules.

Try to identify these groups very early--before you spend money on equipment or services.   Example: some organizations contribute printing; approach them before contracting elsewhere for this work.

8. Create a multiplier effect.

Seek ways to turn contributors into fund solicitors--but carefully, so you don't lose friends.

9. Donated labor.

Look for people who will donate labor, saving you cash: sign painters, photographers, people to build signs and make banners, people who can make posters with the silk screen process (on borrowed equipment).

Donated labor interests the Campaign Manager more than the Finance Committee.

10. Loans.

Loans can solve short-term money problems, particularly when the campaign is being organized.

Two types of loans are involved:

* <u>No-interest personal loans</u> to the Campaign Committee--by the candidate, committee members, or others. Part or all of a loan may be "forgiven"--not repaid. Check FPPC regulations!

* <u>Standard bank loans</u> to the Campaign Committee. These must be repaid--with interest. Usually, they require the personal pledge (credit) of one or more people--the candidate, committee members, or others.

11. Decentralized fundraising.

When campaigning in a large area, like a county, or a city with strong neighborhood or ethnic group identification, decentralize fundraising: form special committees in several areas.

12. Special-purpose fundraising.

On occasion, individuals or groups may offer to finance a specific campaign activity--say a Phone Bank--or an item of campaign material, like a special brochure. Try to accommodate these people, so long as your Campaign Manager retains <u>full control</u> of whatever the financing provides.

13. Slate candidates.

If you are running with one or more people as a slate, your campaign costs can be reduced by sharing certain costs like advertising.

14. Multi-purpose polls.

It may be possible in larger campaigns to finance part of all of a voter survey by sharing the cost with non-political groups. This can be useful to identify voter attitudes on issues and candidates. But protect yourself: be sure the poll results are not distributed publicly without approval of your Steering Committee; why let opponents benefit from what you paid to learn?

CHAPTER 6

CAMPAIGN MATERIALS

Campaign materials: your "window" to the voters.

You cannot meet and talk with all of the voters. At best, you will meet only a small percentage of them.

Thus, campaign materials are an essential means of communicating with voters to...

...expand name recognition.

...reinforce positive images.

...raise money.

...build bases of support.

...discuss issues.

...persuade people to give you their votes.

The purpose of this chapter is to assist you in the selection of your campaign materials; then to suggest how to use them effectively.

A checklist is provided in the Appendix to help in the selection process. As you will note, it contains far more materials than you can probably afford--or would want to use. That's the purpose: to give you choices.

The discussion in this chapter centers on three topics:

* "Ground rules" for selecting, preparing and using campaign materials.

* A description of major items.

* Discussion of materials which can simplify the management of your campaign.

GROUND RULES

1. Be cost-effective.
Compare costs of materials with their communications values so you get the most for your money.

Example: The money for an advertisement in a publication with limited circulation might be better spent for an additional mailing to known supporters or undecided voters.

2. Delegate authority.
As the candidate, be concerned with decisions about the content of printed materials. Leave other decisions to your Campaign Committee.

3. Set priorities.
Produce the most important items first, in the order in which they are needed, i.e. a candidate fact sheet and pledge cards first (or a combination Pledge/Endorsement/Volunteer card); a basic brochure second, etc.

After the basic "must have" items are identified set priorities for producing other materials.

4. Identify the committee.
FPPC rules require identification on printed materials, including envelopes, when 200 or more copies are distributed:

* Committee name and address.

* Committee identification number.

* Name of the Chairman or Treasurer.

* Name and address of the printer.

News media require the same identification, plus "Paid Advertisement" above printed ads and in radio and TV commercials.

Be smart and include a telephone number on printed materials--a number where someone is available.

Check the FPPC manual, media advertising departments and the post office for identification requirements, type sizes, etc.

5. Pick a good committee name.
Select a committee name which inclues your name, as the candidate.

Make the name short enough to fit easily on printed materials, like: Committee to Elect John Doe, or Friends of John Doe.

If you plan to keep the committee (and bank account) alive for another election, avoid using the name of the office or the election date in the committee name.

6. Consider the value of a union "bug" (label).

The "bug" identifies a union shop. This can be important in some areas--at least on brochures and other major items.

7. Establish a color theme.

Identification of your campaign among voters can be improved if you stick with a color or combination of colors on printed materials, signs, posters, etc.

Pick colors which are easy on the eyes, but strong enough to attract attention. Avoid pastels.

8. Get bids on high-cost items.

Get several bids before spending large amounts of money for materials. Also, since some organizations contribute services (like printing) instead of money, be sure these avenues are explored before you spend money for major printed items.

9. Prepare to pay in advance.

Campaigns are a cash-and-carry business. Printers usually require half in advance, half when you take delivery. News media require full payment when you place an order for advertising. Everyone else usually asks for full payment upon delivery.

10. Pay by check; get a receipt.

Pay all campaign expenses by check. Get receipts to complete your records.

11. Make multiple use of materials.

Plan your materials so you can get multiple use if possible, to save both time and money.

Example: Your Statement of Qualifications for the voter pamphlet can also be used as a candidate fact sheet.

Example: Design your brochure as a self-mailer; also for fundraising.

12. Field test materials.

Before you print an item, field test it with a variety of people

31

to see that it is clear and persuasive: campaign workers, friends not involved in the campaign, people who are experts in communications, etc.

13. Attend to production details.

Printers print what you give them, according to whatever instructions you provide. You can avoid costly mistakes by...

...having one person in charge of production.

...providing a layout and complete instructions for type faces, type sizes, placement of pictures, picture sizes, kind and color of paper, ink colors, how items are folded, etc.

...having several people read proof to correct spelling and to see that printers followed instructions.

...giving materials to printers early enough to allow time for proof-reading and corrections.

...The same rules for newspaper ads.

14. Look for price breaks.

The cost of printing goes down (per unit) as the quantity goes up. Discuss with the printer where you get the best deal on quantity.

Also look for other ways to save money, such as reusing old campaign signs, furnishing wood for signs instead of buying it from the sign painter, letting printers substitute lower cost paper, using word processing to set type (instead of a typesetter), having a volunteer (with experience) do pasteups.

CAMPAIGN MATERIALS AND THEIR USES

1. Candidate fact sheet.

This is the first item needed: a one-page summary of your experience, qualifications and views on issues. Use it when you start organizing and fundraising, then replace it with your campaign brochure.

2. Pledge/Endorsement/Volunteer cards.

This is the first printed item to order: cards so people can pledge money, endorse you and volunteer to work--all on one card.

You need them as early as possible to start raising money

and to line up volunteers. While waiting for delivery, use a typewritten substitute, produced quickly and inexpensively by any "instant" print shop.

Order plenty of cards so you and committee members can make widespread distribution at receptions, coffees, while campaigning door-to-door and when soliciting money. Remember, the cost per card goes down as the quantity goes up.

3. Campaign brochure.

This is the centerpiece among campaign materials, the chief means (other than personal contact) of telling people who you are and why they should vote for you.

It is a good idea to review other brochures before you print yours. See if local office-holders have spare copies of their campaign brochures which you can study.

Design the brochure to be attractive and easy to read: good design, good writing, in color if possible, with your picture (face).

Design it as a self-mailer--one panel (after folding) with the campaign committee name and address (and ID) in the upper left-hand corner, space in the center for an address and a bulk mail permit in the upper right-hand corner.

You may not know, when you have the brochure printed, whether you will have money for a mass mailing. But play it safe--be an optimist--and get a mailing permit and print it on the brochure. (Contact your local post office for permit information, rules and costs.)

Order enough copies of the brochure to deliver one to each voter household and have copies available for receptions, coffees, fundraisers, precinct walking, etc.

4. Statement of Qualifications. (Sample in Part II.)

This is a high-priority item: a 200-word summary of your qualifications which you are permitted to file with your nomination papers. It will be published in the pamphlet mailed to registered voters by the County Clerk about three weeks before the election.

Candidates filing statements share the cost of that portion of the pamphlet. It's a bargain because...

...it reaches all registered voters.

...you don't pay postage.

...it is the last item many voters read.

...it's the only campaign material some voters read.

5. Advertisements.

A cost-effective way to reach large numbers of voters is with paid advertising in local newspapers. (Radio and TV are too expensive for most local campaigns.)

There are many uses for advertising...

...to build name recognition early in the campaign.

...to promote campaign events.

...to raise money.

...to debate issues.

...to recruit volunteers.

...to get votes.

Most advertising in typical local campaigns is done in the last few weeks of the campaign. Here's a way to plan a series of three ads for effective results:

* The first ad to "introduce" you to voters: list your qualifications, experience and community activities.

* Use the second ad to discuss issues.

* Make the final ad an appeal for votes. (This is the time to publish names of people and organizations endorsing you.)

Talk with newspaper advertising departments about sizes and shapes. You can dominate a page, for example, without buying a full-page ad.

Consider special-purpose publications when they are cost-effective in reaching voters: senior citizen newspapers, even local high school and college papers.

6. Signs and posters.

Determine how your community reacts to campaign signs and posters before getting into this business. In some areas, they can harm you, in others they are the mainstay of local elections.

Also check local city and county sign ordinances before designing or placing signs and posters.

Signs are usually hand-painted on wood--large (over six square feet, but not billboard size), heavy, requiring a crew to install and remove them.

Posters are printed on cardboard, are smaller, and are used in windows, on lawns, or on stakes along roads.

Use colors which attract attention and are easy to read. Follow the color theme you establish for your campaign.

Place signs and posters along well-traveled routes.

Most cities and counties require a deposit to ensure that signs are removed immediately after elections.

Keep wording to a minimum: their chief value is name identification.

Get permission from owners before putting signs or posters on private property.

7. Advertising inserts.

You can pay newspapers to insert your printed material in their papers for delivery to their customers. You pay for the printing of the material, of course, but sometimes inserts can be cheaper than mailing.

Talk to newspaper advertising departments about sizes and types of inserts. Also consider how many non-voters you will be reaching--and how many throw away this kind of material without reading it.

8. "Dear Friend" cards.

These should be a high-priority item in your campaign: cards larger than standard postcards which your supporters mail to their friends about a week before the election--with a printed message endorsing you.

"Dear Friend" cards are effective: voters telling friends to vote for you.

An essay on how to design and use "Dear Friend" cards is included in Part II of the book.

9. Bumper stickers.

These are effective in promoting your name, but you should consider:

* How effective they are in your community.

* Whether you can get enough people to use them.

* What else you can buy with the same money.

10. **Other materials.**

* News releases: essential--see the essay on news tips in Part II.

* Additional fact sheets: Useful to reach specific groups quickly and inexpensively.

* Flyers: Valuable in promoting events and for last minute advertising (distributed in shopping centers and door-to-door).

* Position papers: Needed in some types of campaigns to elaborate on issues; usually for limited distribution.

* Gimmicks and giveaway items: Not cost-effective in most local campaigns.

ADMINISTRATIVE AND MANAGEMENT MATERIALS

1. **Financial records.**
One fortunate thing about California FPPC regulations is that they specify what forms to use for reporting contributions and expenditures. This makes life easier for treasurers.

2. **Calendars.**

A Master Calendar for the Campaign Manager and Steering Committee--listing dates for all campaign activities.
An Events Calendar for the candidate, Scheduling Chairman and others--listing the candidate's schedule or personal appearances.
Special Calendars for community events, precinct activities, fundraising events, etc.

3. **Schedules.**

Planning Schedules for decision-making.
Production Schedules for campaign materials, events, activities (like Phone Banks).
Work Schedules for volunteers: precinct workers, Phone Bank callers, headquarters staff, election day get-out-the-vote campaign.
Advertising Schedule: dates ads appear in each publication and dates for each preparatory step.

4. **Checklists.**
There is no substitute for checklists to be sure that everything

gets done. An extensive set of campaign checklists is included in the Appendix.

5. Voter lists and labels.

You can order several kinds of voter lists as well as mailing labels from your County Clerk. Allow time for delivery, usually about two weeks.

* Voters listed by street address, within precincts, for precinct work and the get-out-the-vote effort on election day.

* The alphabetical listing by name has limited use, primarily to locate people on your lists.

* Labels should be ordered by households, that is, one label for each family surname.

Voter lists contain telephone numbers of people who include them voluntarily on their voter registration cards. If you plan a Phone Bank and get-out-the-vote campaign, put volunteers to work early to insert missing numbers, using the telephone book or a reverse directory.

6. FPPC forms.

The Fair Political Practices Commission manual and forms are available from City Clerks and County Clerks, as well as from the FPPC offices in Sacramento. It is important that the Campaign Manager and Treasurer read these carefully to avoid problems. (See Chapter 9 for more information.)

7. City and county forms.

Contact both City and County Public Works Departments for forms for sign permits. Order precinct maps, voter lists and mailing labels from the County Clerk. Also, some counties publish a pamphlet with key dates and instructions for candidates for each election.

8. Postal regulations and forms.

Talk with your local postmaster about bulk mail permits, post office boxes for campaigns and regulations governing political campaign mailings. Get the forms and have one person study the regulations--which are complex and confusing at best--so you have an in-house expert on the subject.

CHAPTER 7

FILING
TO RUN

Pay close attention to the rules.

You are a candidate when you complete the filing procedure required by state law.

The procedures vary according to the office you are seeking...

...so visit your City Clerk if you are running for a city office.

...or your County Clerk if you are running for a county or a district office.

...and learn the rules well in advance of the filing date. (Example: The only opportunity to file a Statement of Qualifications is when you file nomination papers.)

The filing period opens about 90 days before the election. It lasts about three weeks.

You **must:**

* Complete forms according to rules governing names, occupations and personal identification.

* Obtain signatures of sponsors--voters eligible to vote for you. The number varies with the office.

* Pay a filing fee for certain offices--an amount which varies with offices--or submit voter signatures in lieu of the fee.

You **may:**

* Submit voter signatures to pay all or part of the filing fee.

* File a Statement of Qualifications (maximum 200 words) to be published in the pamphlet mailed to voters by the County Clerk about three weeks before the election.

You **can:**

* Benefit from publicity when you take out papers or when you file them--or both, if you are clever.

* Generate interest (and support) for your campaign by announcing your candidacy in advance of the opening of the filing period.

* Begin organizing your campaign as early as you wish. BUT if you collect or spend $500 you or your committee must register with the (California) Secretary of State--and this makes your candidacy public.

DECISIONS TO MAKE

1. **When to start organizing.**
Obviously, the earlier you start, the more time you have and, presumably, the better job you will do.

2. **When to announce.**
This is a strategy decision. If you announce early, you might discourage others from entering the race, especially if you are a strong candidate.
Announcing late can have some advantages. You know who else is in the race, and issues may be clearer.

3. **How to announce.**
Hold a news conference...or simply issue a news release...or do it at a small reception...or plan a large kickoff and fundraising event...or do nothing but file nomination papers.

4. **Statement of Qualifications.**
The opportunity to reach all voters with your message is far too valuable to ignore. If funds are limited, this might be your only chance to get your story to all the voters.

If you are not yet organized, pay the cost of the Statement yourself; then be reimbursed when there is money in your campaign treasury.

In writing your Statement, you will probably want to state your views on major issues. This can be difficult when you must write weeks before the campaign begins. Think carefully about what you say; you're stuck with the positions you take.

5.   Signatures in lieu of fees.
You can save money using this option. Also, people who sign this petition tend to support you throughout the campaign. In addition, you can glean favorable publicity by submitting a long list of voter names at this early date.

6.   A last-minute decision to run.
You may be undecided whether to run in this election. But if very few people file, be prepared to make a last-minute decision to file. In some races, when at least one incumbent fails to file for re-election by the close of the filing period, the period is extended five calendar days for everyone <u>except</u> incumbents. This gives you another few days to act.

HANDLING THE NEWS MEDIA

Most local newspapers try to publish a fairly long story on each candidate entering a race. This is done at filing time. You can enhance news coverage in several ways:

* Provide written news releases.
Editors--and their readers--are interested in who you are, your community affiliations and your campaign platform. Give them this information in a simple, straightforward news release: typed, double-spaced, on one side of a sheet of paper containing your name, address and telephone number. Deliver the news release yourself, if possible, so editors and reporters have an opportunity to meet you and ask questions. This way, you become a person, instead of just a name.

* Provide a photograph.
Papers publish only pictures of candidates' faces. Give them a good clear picture--black and white, either 8x10 or

5x7 inches. If necessary, invest in a professional photographer, then use the same picture in your campaign material.

* Be available for interviews.

Many local editors like to have their reporters interview candidates, rather than to work only from a news release.

* Prepare yourself carefully!

It's like the line in movies: "Anything you say can be taken down and used against you." Reporters will ask all kinds of questions; be careful with your answers! Don't say anything you don't want to see in print.

* Observe deadlines.

If there are daily and weekly papers in your area, pick a date for the news release which gives both types of papers an even break.

CHAPTER 8

CAMPAIGNING

Keep your eye on the target: votes!

Campaigning begins, in a sense, when you decide to run and you start lining up people and money. All of the organizing and fundraising efforts are part of campaigning.

This chapter concerns the last four to six weeks before the election, the period when voters begin to get interested and the news media start to pay attention.

You must realize that long campaigns bore voters. Many of them don't give an election serious thought until they receive their sample ballots in the mail--about three weeks before election day. Thus, you can waste time, money and effort by starting to campaign too early.

There is no official date when campaigns begin. However, by custom--and this varies with communities and offices--most local campaigns get into high gear about a month before election day. We are concerned here with what you and your committee do during these crucial weeks.

This chapter deals with three topics:

* General approaches to campaigning.

* Specific campaign activities.

* A list of hints and options.

GENERAL APPROACHES

1. Pacing.

Pace your efforts--you and your campaign committee--to build momentum so your campaign "peaks" just before the election. You want a flurry of activity at the end.

Pacing also includes dividing your campaign into phases:

...the early phase to expand name recognition.

...the mid-period to discuss issues.

...the final 10-14 days to appeal for votes.

2. Grass roots campaigning.

Take the campaign to the voters in their own homes--with plenty of personal contact.

3. Cultivate pockets of votes.

Research can identify neighborhoods and groups where you have solid support. Concentrate effort on these "pockets" to consolidate and expand your support.

4. Flexibility.

Things happen fast in campaigns. When opportunities arise, capitalize on them. Be an opportunist.

5. Use the media to advantage.

The news media reach more people in a day than you can reach in weeks of knocking on doors. Be cooperative. Learn to create news.

(An essay on news tips is included in Part II.)

CAMPAIGN ACTIVITIES

1. The kickoff.

Select a date about a month before the election for your official "kickoff." Make this an event to generate publicity--and a rally for campaign workers.

Don't worry about the fact that you may have had an announcement party weeks or months earlier, or that you have held several fundraising events. The media and the public will respond to this "official" beginning of serious campaigning.

2. Coffees.

Coffees may begin well before the campaign kickoff, but the number and frequency should increase during the early part of the campaign period.

3. Precinct walking.

As a candidate, your job is to walk door-to-door to meet voters. Members of your precinct organization also participate, delivering campaign materials.

Avoid long discussions. The objective is to meet as many voters as possible.

4. Endorsements.

Solicit endorsements from individuals and organizations--then publicize them. The name of any organization and any prominent person endorsing you is news.

You may use names of endorsers in ads late in the campaign--a decision which depends on how many names you collect, money available and your advertising strategy. Nevertheless, collect all the endorsements you can, starting even before the campaign period begins.

5. Public appearances.

Use every opportunity to speak before groups or merely to be introduced as a candidate.

A variety of opportunities will arise:

* Candidate forums.

These are events, common in most communities, where one or more local groups sponsor a public event to give all candidates an opportunity to be heard.

* Organization meetings.

Some organizations, including colleges, invite one candidate per meeting to speak for a few minutes; some invite all candidates to speak for a limited time (2-5 minutes).

Also plan to have friends invite you as a guest to their organizations' meetings, just to be introduced (and, of course, to meet and talk to members before and after the meeting).

* **Public and private functions.**

Attend any public or private function where you have an opportunity to shake hands with voters. As a time-saver, you may want to limit your time at these affairs: move about the room quickly to meet as many people as possible, then leave. You may be able to attend several events in one evening this way.

* **TV and radio.**

Depending upon the area and race, radio and TV stations may give candidates opportunities on the air; look for local cable companies which offer opportunities.

6. **News media opportunities.**

Local newspapers often use three systems for giving candidates an opportunity to express their views:

* **Open space:** a designated number of words per candidate to say whatever they wish. All statements are usually published at one time.

* **Questions:** all candidates are given the same set of questions and a word limit for responses. These are also published as a group.

* **Interviews:** one or more reporters are assigned to interview candidates. Usually, the major issues will be discussed with all candidates. But reporters may also dig deeper on some subjects with some candidates. The results of the interviews may be published at one time, or spaced over a period of days or weeks.

News media usually cover most public events involving candidates, like candidates' nights and debates. You can improve your coverage by providing reporters with written statements.

7. **Special events.**

Imagination and energy are the only limits on the kinds of events your campaign committee can plan--picnics, spaghetti feeds, ball games, dances, parades, auto caravans, human billboards, headquarters open house...anything to attract crowds and publicity.

8. **Phone Banks; get-out-the-vote campaigns.**

Three or four weeks before the election, volunteers call all registered voters to identify your supporters. They mark the voter sheets, then, on election day, volunteers call known supporters to remind them to vote (if they haven't voted by about 4 p.m.). (See the essays on these subjects in Part II.)

9. Publicity.
This is a continuing effort--but shape it to the needs and desires of local editors!

Some editors place restrictions on the types and amounts of publicity material they will use, including letters to the editors. Play by the rules or you waste time and get editors mad at you.

10. Advertising.
Advertising is so expensive that in most local campaigns it is saved for the last few days in daily papers and the last three or four weeks in weekly papers.

As a suggestion, divide your ads into three groups, the same way you phase other campaign activities:

* Early ads identify your name and qualifications.

* Mid-period ads discuss issues.

* Final ads solicit votes, including names of endorsers.

As a tip for making friends with publishers, don't discriminate; if you advertise in one local paper, put ads in all of them (but not necessarily the same size ads).

11. Mailings.
Direct mail is an effective way to reach voters. The problem is the cost for printing and postage.

As an alternative to mass mailings to all voter households, you might consider selective mailing, either to known supporters--to get them out to vote--or to undecided groups.

12. Signs and posters.
Do what is appropriate in your community in using campaign signs and posters. This is a committee function.

13. "Dear Friend" cards.
Volunteers mail cards to their friends, asking them to vote for you--one of the last-minute activities in the campaign. An essay in Part II tells you how to plan and organize this activity.

HINTS AND OPTIONS

About spouses and families.

Involve all members of your immediate family in the decision to run...be sure they understand the time and stresses involved in campaigning...make certain you have their full support.

Keep spouses out of the decision-making process: they are naturally biased in their opinions of you.

Spouses and families are most helpful when they make your home life comfortable and are involved only in social events during the campaign.

Your appearance and actions.

...keep hair clean and neat...a flattering, but not distracting style...easy to maintain...out of your eyes.

...dress appropriately for each occasion...comfortable...in good taste...not too flashy.

...develop good speaking habits...clarity...brevity...eye contact...use a coach if necessary.

...avoid (or cure) distracting mannerisms.

...go easy on alcoholic beverages.

Scheduling your time.

This is your committee's responsibility...be sure to have them include rest periods.

Criticism.

Learn to take criticism from your Steering Committee. Invite them to be blunt.

As for opponents, ignore their comments.

But voters...listen carefully!

Meeting people.

You act first--introduce yourself with a smile and an outstretched hand.

Remember, some people are nervous when strangers approach them. Being relaxed and friendly can defuse the situation.

Learn to remember names!

Spend more time listening than talking. Remember your goal: votes.

Campaigning hints:

* If you are new at the game, start precinct-walking close to home, where you know people. Expand your areas as you begin to feel more comfortable.

* Carry spare shoes and socks in your car; change frequently to refresh your feet and legs.

* Stop precinct-walking before you are over-tired.

* <u>Never</u> speak harshly about opponents: their records, yes; their personalities, no.

* Answer all questions. If you don't know the facts, say so--and offer to get answers, then call back with answers.

* Be clear and logical in your positions. Voters hate candidates who are wishy-washy.

* Don't make promises you can't keep--such as what you will do if elected, when everyone knows it takes a majority of the board to take action.

Say "Thank you" frequently.

Thank volunteers repeatedly throughout the campaign for their work--or their offer to work.

Call and thank people who host events for you--then follow up immediately with a hand-written note.

Thank voters and committee members for ideas.

About personal problems.

If there is anything in your past--personal, professional or political--which may arise to cause problems, plan in advance to handle the situation quickly and firmly. Discuss these problems with your Steering Committee very early in your campaign. Ask their advice.

If personal problems arise during the campaign, seek help from your Steering Committee immediately.

Avoid allowing personal problems with no political implications to interfere with your campaigning.

Keep abreast of the news.

When you are a candidate--no matter what office--some people think you know more than you really do about affairs which have nothing to do with the election. The best solution is to read news summaries daily, if possible, and have committee members fill you in on events you might be asked about.

Campaigning options:

* **Tracking polls:** Have volunteers make random calls to registered voters periodically to see how you stand in relation to other candidates. The simplest system is to have them call every 20th or 25th name on the voter list.

* **Classified ads:** Use some of your advertising money for ads in the classified sections of newspapers for short messages and name awareness.

* **Letters to the editors:** If local editors accept letters from or about candidates, plan a campaign to have letters from supporters submitted--but target specific topics or issues.

* **Auto caravans:** Have your committee organize them late in the campaign to drive through residential neighborhoods and local shopping centers--decorated with signs and banners, maybe even using a public address system.

* **Human billboards:** Organize groups of volunteers to work on election day--at the morning and evening commute hours--as human billboards: each person carrying a large card with a word or a letter, so the group spells out a message: VOTE FOR JOHN DOE.

* **Write a newspaper column:** Buy space in your local newspaper and write a weekly or semi-weekly column about local issues and problems. This must be identified as a paid political ad, of course. But it is an effective way to communicate with voters. Use a space about two columns wide and five inches deep. This is enough for about 500 words per column.

AND THE FINAL WORD...

There's no such thing as "time off" during a campaign! If you want to be elected, give all your time to the campaign. Keep your eye on the target: votes!

CHAPTER 9

CAMPAIGN REPORTS

**Campaign reporting is a necessity.
Put your Treasurer in charge.**

The (California) Political Reform Act of 1974 establishes financial reporting requirements and other controls on your campaign, among them:

* Candidates, individuals or committees which collect or spend $500 must register.

* Every campaign must have a Treasurer.

* Reports of contributions and expenditures must be made during and after the campaign.

* Committees (or other sponsors) must be identified on campaign materials and in advertisements.

* Contributors of $100 or more must be identified.

* Cash contributions are limited.

* Certain candidates and <u>all</u> elected officials must file personal financial disclosure reports.

As a first step, go to your City, Clerk, County Clerk, or local Registrar of Voters and get a copy of the current year **Information Manual on Campaign Disclosure Provisions of the Political Reform Act.** Also get copies of the forms you need for your type of campaign and reporting requirement.
Read the Manual carefully. Make sure your Campaign Manager, Treasurer and Finance Chairman also read it.
There are legal and financial penalites for failing to follow the rules--and potential political embarrassment too.
Next, have your Treasurer register your Campaign Committee and get an Identification Number (ID#) if you have received or spent $500--or even if you **think** you will receive or spend $500 during the campaign.

Be aware that the law and procedures governing campaign reporting change frequently--as the result of legislative action, court decisions or FPPC administrative decisions. Don't use out-of-date manuals and forms. And don't hesitate to ask for help.

You can get help on reporting and disclosure requirements from several sources:

* Your City Clerk (on city elections).

* Your County Clerk/Registrar of Voters (for county and special district elections).

* The FPPC offices in Sacramento or Los Angeles (on any matter covered by the Political Reform Act). The FPPC will accept collect calls: Sacramento (916) 322-5662 or Los Angeles (213) 620-5196.

Reporting requirements may also affect campaign decisions:

* **Personal financial disclosure requirements** cause some would-be candidates to hesitate before entering races.

* **The $500 trigger** for registering your commitee is a tactical problem. You may want to slow down fundraising and spending, or advance your announcement date.

* **Timing receipt of certain contributions** is another tactical consideration: defer some contributions until after a mid-campaign reporting date so you don't tip off other candidates on how much money you have.

* **Limiting contributions from certain sources** sometimes results when candidates want to avoid being too heavily identified with an interest group.

* **Design of campaign material and advertisements** to include the Campaign Committee name and ID#.

Overall, reporting and other requirements are not difficult to understand. It does not require a professional accountant to complete the financial reports, nor a lawyer to follow the other rules. But it does require attention to details to avoid problems.

In a sense, the financial reporting requirements provide a useful service to candidates and their communities. They give you a ready-made bookkeeping system so you always know your financial status.

PART II

ESSAYS AND SAMPLES

Building Name Recognition

One of the first steps in a campaign is to make your name known to as many people as possible. After that, you can work on persuading them to vote for you.

We all enjoy a degree of name recognition as a result of our business, social and civic activities. However, that recognition is usually limited to a few segments of the total voting community. Therefore, you must take stock of the situation and decide a course of action.

Here is one approach to the subject:

* **Inventory community constituencies.**

Identify groups held together by common bonds and their own internal communications system. One example is a Chamber of Commerce--a common bond and good internal communications. Other constituencies would include homeowner associations, church groups, service and fraternal organizations, conservation and environmental groups, parent associations (both elementary and high school levels), perhaps the "country club set," even the so-called "old" families in town.

*   Identify friendly constituencies.
    This begins with groups in which you are a member or share interests (like the PTA, if you have children in school).   But it goes farther.   Try to identify (and list) groups of people who would be inclined to support you because of your background, views, interests, community projects, or for other reasons.

*   Select constituencies to penetrate.
    Essentially, this is a task of rating constituencies according to their size and influence in your community. Suppose, for example, that candidates who are endorsed by the merchants association always seem to win elections.   Or, perhaps, endorsement by a federation of homeowner associations means victory.   This would identify the merchants association (or homeowner federation) as one of the major constituencies to penetrate.   Conversely, you might rule out some local conservation organizations if their membership is small and they don't seem to carry weight with the majority of voters.

Having done your research and planning, how you proceed depends to some extent on how much time remains before your election.   Obviously, if you have six months or more before the election, you can do things which would be impossible if you had only a month or two.
    These are some things to do to increase name recognition, assuming you have a reasonable amount of time:

1.   Become more active in organizations.
    In organizations in which you are already a member, attend meetings regularly, participate in projects, circulate so that all members get to know you.

2.   Seek out leadership opportunities.
    Look for opportunities to move into leadership positions within organizations and the community, without committing yourself to an excessive amount of time.   Sometimes friends can help by suggesting that you head a committee, a task force or be the spokesman for organizations.

3. **Visit new organizations.**

Ask friends to take you along as a guest to their organizations. Make an effort to meet as many people as possible.

4. **Circulate in the community.**

Move about in the community, attending as many diverse functions as possible. If you have children in school, attend school functions, athletic events, music and theater presentations, meetings of parents. Even if you don't have children, you can become a merit badge counselor for Boy Scouts or Girl Scouts. Watch local newspapers for announcements of civic events which are open to the public and attend them.

5. **Attend meetings of government agencies.**

It is especially important to attend meetings of the government agency to which you want to be elected. This is part of the learning process, to understand how the agency operates, what problems it faces and to get an idea of what you would do as an elected member of the Board.

6. **Speak out on issues.**

Use every opportunity available to speak out on issues of concern to the community. Do this at meetings of organizations, at public hearings of government agencies, even as a programmed speaker if possible. Prepare yourself before you speak. Spend time studying issues and what they mean to the community, along with developing a point of view which will carry over when you begin to speak as a candidate. As an example, if you are running for the school board, start speaking out on issues affecting the quality of education, management of the school system, crime, discipline, or any number of topics.

7. **Write letters to editors.**

It is relatively easy to have your letters printed in the local newspaper if you write on topics of general community interest. Make your letters short and to the point: About 100 words, never over 200. Write so that each letter makes a point that readers will remember.

8. **Have friends respond to your letters.**

Arrange with friends to respond to your letters saying, in effect, "(your name) makes sense." This helps to build name recognition.

9. Ask to write guest editorials.

Some editors invite local residents to write guest editorials on subjects of interest to the community. These run 300 words or more and require good writing to hold reader interest. Editors usually pick guest writers on the basis of their knowledge of a particular subject. Thus, you want to pick a topic you are qualified to write about before you approach the editor.

10. Buy space and write a column.

You can do a quick job of building name recognition by buying space in your local paper and writing a weekly column.

In one instance, a candidate for city council became well-known in a period of 8 weeks for the cost of a half a page of advertising in his local weekly newspaper.

Starting when he filed nomination papers (about 3 months before the election), he bought space every week, two columns wide and 5" deep.

He titled his column, "Door-to-Door With (his name)" and wrote about things people told him about how to improve city government. Each week he went into a different area and asked residents what they saw as the major problems facing the community and what they would like to see the City Council do to solve them.

He was elected to one of the three open seats in a field of eight candidates.

11. Conduct your own survey.

Take a clip board, a set of questions and a notebook and conduct your own survey of voter attitudes on community issues.

Evenings and weekends walk through neighborhoods in various parts of the community, asking voters their opinions.

You may want to identify yourself as a possible candidate for office, or simply as an interested citizen trying to find ways to improve life in the community.

Naturally, you want everyone you meet to remember your name, so you may want to carry a business card to give to people, or a list of printed questions with an invitation for people to answer them and mail them back to you.

If you are going to go to this effort, make use of the information: Use it in speeches for local groups, when you speak out at government agency hearings, in letters to Editors or in guest editorials. In addition to getting name recognition, you learn what's on the minds of voters.

12. Seek publicity opportunities.

The more often your name appears in the newspapers the more people will recognze it. This is plain common sense. The problem is how to generate personal publicity.

This can be done in several ways:

* When you speak out at meetings of public agencies, make your comments clear, concise and to the point so they are easy for reporters to remember. Also, provide written copies of your comments for reporters.

* When you are appointed to an office or committee in an organization, ask the group to issue a news release. If this is not possible, call the newspaper yourself.

* If your local newspaper has a column with short items about local people, call the columnist with items. It is a curious fact, but the more often your name appears in print, the easier it becomes to get into print.

* If you are going to launch a project of interest to the community, sit down with your local editor or reporter and describe the project and what it means to the community. Then follow up with progress reports.

Advice for Campaign Managers

Don't worry about titles. You may be called Campaign Chairman, Campaign Manager, Coordinator or something else. In any case, you are in charge of the campaign. The candidate looks to you for help and the volunteers expect leadership and direction.

Establish a clear relationship with the candidate at the outset: he or she makes the initial decisions about campaign style, policies and positions on major issues; you run the show, including keeping the candidate on track.

If there is no Steering Committee, form one. Use this group in the decision-making process on the basis that several heads are better than one. Include the Treasurer, Finance Chairman and Precinct or Volunteer Chairman and then add a few more people for their knowledge of campaigns, issues or the community.

Establish regular meeting times for the Steering Committee, perhaps every two or three weeks if the election is several months away; once a week or more frequently during the campaign. Use these meetings to bring everyone up to date on campaign finances, fundraising, planning and other activities; discuss problems and make decisions.

Learn to delegate responsibility. Trust the people heading various action committees, such as fundraising, precinct work, coffees, etc. But work with them individually, giving advice when necessary and prodding from time to time so deadlines are met.

Approach your job in an organized manner:

1. Get a clear picture of what needs to be done.

2. Establish priorities.

3. Assign responsibilities.

4. Organize a management system which fits your needs: reports, records, charts, meetings, schedules, deadlines.

5. Anticipate problems before they arise.

6. Keep a cool head.

These are some of the problems you will encounter and ways for dealing with them:

Handling Money.

Avoid waste, mishandling and other problems by establishing tight controls:

* Limit the Finance Committee to raising money.

* The Treasurer banks the money, pays the bills and files FPPC reports.

* You, as Campaign Manager, allocate money and approve spending.

* The candidate does not handle money, except to receive checks and turn them over to the Treasurer.

* If you use a Budget Committee, its job is to allocate funds among activities but, you retain authority to shift funds within limits.

Confidentiality.

It is imperative that campaign plans and serious problems be kept in strict confidence among as few people as possible: you, the candidate and the Steering Committee at most. Don't give opponents unnecessary advantages.

Ringers.

It is not uncommon in some campaigns for opponents to have their friends join your campaign organization as spies. Usually they leave when they are discovered, but you need to be alert.

Reliability.

Volunteers are great people, but they are not always reliable. Some take on more than they can handle, some are distracted by personal, family and job problems. Learn to spot problems.

Too Many Experts.

Almost everyone who gets involved in a campaign is something of an "expert" on what influences voters. Don't discourage this feeling: channel it to productive uses.

Over-reaction.

Unexpected events occur in every campaign: sometimes a disaster; at other times an opponent scores a coup. There is a tendency at these times for people to panic. Even Steering Committee members may over-react. Keep cool. Just analyze the situation calmly and do whatever is necessary.

Fatigue.

Learn to spot signs of fatigue among campaign workers, committee members and the candidate. The tension and steady work during the busy periods of a campaign takes its toll on everyone. Sometimes a simple "day off" or a party for campaign volunteers is the answer. Or, if you are good at it, an old-fashioned pep talk will do the job.

The candidate.

The candidate can give managers two kinds of problems: either paying too much attention to details or not paying enough attention to what is going on. The answer is to take him or her aside for a frank discussion.

The Care & Feeding of Volunteers

Advice for Volunteer Coordinators

No campaign can function without volunteers--and the more you have the better.

You must rely on volunteer help for what seems like a million chores: from big jobs, like distributing materials door-to-door, to tiresome small chores like converting lists of people into card files.

One of the most important and most difficult jobs in any campaign is being the volunteer in charge of volunteers. This essay on the care and feeding of volunteers is written primarily for you.

Your title is not important: Volunteer Coordinator, Precinct Chairman, whatever.

What is important is that you are a diplomat, a firm but fair boss, have a sense of humor and a cool head, be well-organized and, above all, can handle an incredible amount of detail without getting flustered.

WHERE VOLUNTEERS COME FROM

Volunteers come from a few obvious sources, like the candidate's family and close friends. They also come from a variety of unlikely sources, and one of your jobs is to discover them.

Here are some places to find volunteers:

* **Perpetual volunteers.**

    In every community, there are people who like the fun and excitement of working in campaigns. All they need is to be asked. One way to spot them is to check lists of volunteers who have worked in previous campaigns.

* **Retired people.**

    This is a group with the time available and all kinds of valuable experience which can be put to use in a campaign. But be prepared to convince them that working as a volunteer does not require special training, nor that it will take more time than they are willing to give.

60

* **The Candidate's "constituency."**

Every candidate has some kind of constituency in the community: members of organizations and interest groups, social circles, other types of contacts in the area. Each of these groups is a source of volunteers.

* **Volunteers.**

One of the best sources of volunteers is volunteers. Ask them to recruit friends as one of their first tasks.

TIPS FOR RECRUITING VOLUNTEERS

1. **Ask them.**

Very few people volunteer on their own; the vast majority want to be asked.

2. **Make the job sound easy.**

A great majority of volunteers have no previous experience in political campaigns, even though they may have done other kinds of volunteer work. Fear can make them reluctant, unless you explain that the job is really quite easy. To do this, of course, you have to talk in terms of specific activities.

3. **Describe the fun involved.**

Campaigns are a lot of fun. Make a point of telling prospective volunteers about the fun they will have working with a group of good-natured people, doing interesting and exciting things.

4. **Have people recruit their friends.**

Most people who volunteer do so because friends asked them. The good thing about a friend-to-friend recruiting program is that you create a chain letter effect and relieve yourself of work.

HINTS FOR WORKING WITH VOLUNTEERS

* **Explain jobs carefully.**

Take time to explain what is expected and how long each job will take.

* **Make every job sound important.**

Volunteers do better work and are happier when they feel that what they are doing is important. Take time, or have committee chairmen take time to point out what each task means in terms of the overall campaign.

* Keep them busy.

Give volunteers work to do; otherwise they will quit and go away. Sometimes, it doesn't matter so much <u>what</u> you ask them to do, as long as you keep them <u>busy</u>.

* Fit assignments to people.

Give volunteers jobs they are equipped to do and willing to undertake.

You will discover that most men drift towards the financial end of the campaign or physical work, like putting up signs and posters. Women usually prefer office work and telephoning. But there are exceptions: retired men, for example, sometimes prefer routine tasks and detail work.

* Be sure volunteers know what is expected of them.

Life is easier for everyone when written instructions and deadlines are provided.

* Create working teams.

Volunteers often feel more comfortable when they work in teams. For example, in distributing materials door-to-door, send volunteers out in pairs. They enjoy the job more when they keep one another company. This team approach is particularly important--and productive--on big jobs, like putting mailing labels on campaign literature.

* Consider personal preferences.

Most volunteers have definite ideas about things they will or will not do. Example: Some people dislike telephone work; others refuse to go door-to-door. Keep these individual preferences in mind when you make assignments.

* Match assignments to volunteer time available.

A few volunteers have unlimited time to give to the campaign. However, the majority have other responsibilities which limit their time. Thus, with time-consuming tasks, either find someone with time available or break jobs up so several people can complete them.

* Let some volunteers work at home.

Women with small children and others may be willing to work at home when they can't work at headquarters. Try to accomodate them. Example: Inserting telephone numbers on precinct sheets; making name tags.

* **Watch for "big talkers."**

    A few people always do a better job of talking than working. All you can do is to be careful with assignments.

* **Spot the few "super achievers."**

    Try to spot the volunteers who always do more than what is expected of them. These are real gems; they thrive on work. But be careful not to overload them.

* **Establish a headquarters.**

    Volunteers tend to accomplish more when they work at a "campaign headquarters." In big campaigns this is no problem; space can be rented. In small campaigns, you can create a "headquarters" in one person's home (the candidate's, the Campaign Manager's, yours, someone else's). This gives volunteers a sense of stability.

* **Get volunteers involved.**

    Volunteers do better work when they are deeply involved in events, like a campaign kick-off: one group working on decorations, another on food, another handling invitations, another on clean-up. Make them feel it is their event.

* **Create morale-building situations.**

    You need to take time out from campaigning to work on volunteers' morale, like a potluck dinner midway in the campaign.

* **Don't make volunteers spend their money on campaign business.**

    They don't mind contributing to the campaign, but they resent having to pay out of their own pockets for small supply items, lunch when they are doing campaign business and other miscellaneous expenses.

* **Say "Thank You" frequently.**

    It is extremely important to thank volunteers for each job they do. Recognition for their work is about the only reward they get, other than self-satisfaction.

* **Create a social atmosphere whenever possible.**

    One reward in a campaign--other than winning the election--is the social atmosphere. Look for ways to enhance this feeling, such as putting a crew together to do a job even if it is something that two people working alone could accomplish in less time. Example: Putting labels on envelopes or addressing invitations for an event, working at someone's home in the afternoon.

* **Plan for election night.**
     The entire campaign points to just one thing: election day. Plan something for that evening so volunteers can all be together to celebrate the victory. Refreshments are a legitimate campaign expense, so be sure there is money in the budget.

A list of jobs for volunteers is provided in the Appendix.

RECRUIT VOLUNTEERS

Endorsement Programs

Endorsements by individuals and organizations are important enough to receive special attention:

* People usually vote for candidates they endorse. Some also become contributors and campaign workers.

* Organizations encourage members to support candidates they endorse.

* Publicity about endorsements can create a band-wagon effect in the final weeks of the campaign.

* Names of endorsers can be used in ads, flyers, brochures, speeches.

* Endorsers may sponsor coffees, receptions, fundraisers.

* Endorser lists are valuable for direct mail appeals for money, workers and votes.

* News media endorsements influence many voters.

ORGANIZING A PROGRAM

Appoint an Endorsement Chairman, or at least a person to keep records of individuals and groups endorsing you.

Provide space on financial pledge cards for people to give permission to use their names in advertising and publicity. Also provide space for their addresses, telephone numbers and signatures. (Get signatures for your protection.)

Design sign-in sheets used at coffees, receptions and other events with space to indicate an endorsement.

Consider making special sheets, like petitions, to collect endorsements while campaigning door-to-door and in shopping centers.

List organizations and news media to be asked for endorsements. Learn the procedures each group requires.

Prepare to make lists or card files of endorsers.

RUNNING A PROGRAM

Start gathering endorsements when you begin raising money and recruiting volunteers. Keep at it to the end of the campaign. Don't worry about endorsements coming in after the last advertising deadline; every endorsement is a vote.

Contact organizations and editors. Be prepared to be interviewed at length.

Remember, some organizations consider endorsements at the same time they decide on contributions or in-kind services.

Involve committee members and volunteers to help gather endorsements.

USING ENDORSEMENTS

The Campaign Manager and Steering Committee decide how and when to use endorsements. Their decisions depend upon how many endorsements are received, the importance of the individuals and groups, the nature of the community, campaign strategy and how much money is available for advertising and printing.

Some things for managers and committees to consider are:

* Long lists in ads just before the election are impressive.

* Short lists of prominent people and groups are also effective in ads.

* Ads can be split, one portion for names, another for the candidate's qualifications.

* Endorsements carry more weight in some communities than in others.

However endorsements are used, they deserve attention as a means of building support. The nice thing is that an endorsement program does not require a lot of money or people.

"Dear Friend" Cards

Imagine how you would react to a postcard from a friend a few days before an election with a message like this:

> "Please join me in voting for John Doe for City Council next Tuesday, April 6. We need John's business experience to bring some common sense into City government. You will do yourself and our town a favor by voting for John on April 6." (signed) Jim Green.

The chances are that you would be impressed. Someone you know and respect thinks highly enough of John Doe to send you a card. It might just persuade you to vote for him.

That's what "Dear Friend" cards are about: personal endorsements from voters to other voters. They work, and you may pick up just enough extra votes to win.

PREPARATION AND CONTROL ARE THE KEYS.

You need one volunteer to take on this project and follow it through; someone with time to organize and prepare; and with controls to see that everything is done on schedule.

Preparation should start six to eight weeks before the election. This is when you decide the wording and how many cards to print. Then, as quickly as possible, get them printed and in the hands of volunteers to address them to their friends and sign them.

A control system is necessary to be sure that all cards given out are returned so they can all go in the mail about a week before the election.

THE CARDS

* The message must be brief to be effective.

Focus on one or two strong attributes of the candidate and make an appeal for votes. Sometimes issues dictate the message such as: "John Doe is the answer to our crime problem. He supports reorganization of the police department."

* **Size is important:**
Make the card larger than a standard post card, but not so large that extra postage is required. Check with the post office on sizes and with a printer for a size that is economical for him to produce.

* **Colored paper captures readers' attention without adding significantly to the cost.**

* **Decide whether to print one side or both.**

* **Printing one side:**
Message, address and postage are together. The message is on the left side of the card; the address and postage are on the right. The reverse side is blank.

* **Printing two sides:**
Naturally, it costs more to print two sides of a card, but you gain some advantages:
You can print the message, address and postage on one side and the candidate's qualifications, picture, or other material on the reverse side. Or, you can put the address and postage on one side and the message on the reverse.

* **Identification is required.**
California law (FPPC regulations) requires that a mailing of 200 or more pieces of the same item (even if they are not all mailed at one time) must show the name, address and ID number of the committee, with the name of the Chairman or Treasurer. Also, the printer's name and address must be on the card.

POSTAGE - PREPAID OR NOT.
The cost of the campaign is lower if people who sign cards also pay the postage. However, many people will sign fewer cards if they have to pay to mail them.

A third class bulk mail permit costs less than first class mail, but delivery is slower.

A first class permit on the cards speeds up delivery, but detracts slightly from the appearance.

The best looking arrangement, with the quickest delivery, is with first class stamps, paid for by the Campaign Committee and applied by volunteers.

If money is a problem, have the bulk mail permit printed in the upper right hand corner of the cards. Make sure that everyone signing them understands that they must be returned to you to be mailed all at one time. The post office will not accept mailings of less than 200 at one time if you use a third class bulk permit.

QUANTITY.

The number of cards you have printed depends in part on your budget and in part on the number of volunteers who are willing to sign cards.

Your decision has to be made early in the campaign, even before you are sure how many volunteers you will have several weeks later to sign them.

All you can do is make a guess: plan to have 50 cards for each committee member; then add 50% to the total, hoping to find more volunteers when the time comes to sign cards.

INSTRUCTIONS FOR VOLUNTEERS.

Give people written instructions when they receive a batch of cards to sign so they do the job correctly. These are the points to cover:

* The purpose of "Dear Friend" cards.

* How the system works, i.e., volunteers address and sign cards and return them to the committee for mailing.

* How individuals can develop their own list of names, using their Christmas card list, organization rosters and other lists of friends in the community.

* Stress the importance of returning all cards (signed and unsigned) to the volunteer in charge of the program.

* Specific instructions: the name of the contact to get more cards; when and where to turn them in.

CONTROLS.

Chairman and volunteers.

Find one person to take charge of the "Dear Friend" program. Identify several more volunteers to help.

Roster of people to sign cards.

List the name, address and telephone number of everyone who will address and sign cards: campaign committee members, financial contributors, campaign workers, people who signed cards offering to work in the campaign, friends of any of the above, any other people who can be recruited for the program.

Set up a control sheet.

Use any form you wish, but make sure you have names of people who agree to sign cards, how many they received and a column to indicate that the signed cards have been returned to the committee. A sample sheet is at the end of Part II with other sample campaign materials.

Package cards and instructions.

Make up packages of about 25 cards and instructions, held together with a rubber band. This simplifies accounting.

Establish a timetable.

"Dear Friend" cards are most effective when they arrive a few days before the election. Because elections are on Tuesdays you want cards to arrive the previous Friday, Saturday or Monday. To do this, you need a timetable for each step along the way:

* **Four weeks before the election:**
  Hand out cards and instructions with a two-week deadline for people to address and sign them (in ink).

* **Two weeks before the election:**
  All the cards should be addressed, signed and in the hands of the volunteer chairman. Call people and get the missing cards in.

* **Allow a day or two to check cards:**
  Be sure they all have a name, street address, city and zip code. (If your election is entirely within one zip code area, the city and zip code can be printed on the card, saving volunteers time and effort.)

* **Use this checking period to bundle signed cards by zip code.**
  This is a post office requirement for third class mail.

* **About one week before the election, mail the cards:**
  Check with the post office on bulk mail regulations.

Polls, Surveys & Phone Banks

If you want to know what the voters think, ask them.

That's what polls and surveys are about: measuring public opinion.

Phone banks are different: they use survey techniques, but the objective is to identify your supporters.

Professional polls and surveys (we use the terms interchangeably here) are far too expensive for most local campaigns. However, you can adapt professional methods to create home-made surveys which are valuable.

HOW SURVEYS ARE CONDUCTED

It is impractical and expensive to try to contact all voters to get their opinions. However, you can get results which are about 95% accurate by contacting a small percentage of the population, provided you use a scientific system for selecting people to call. This is called random selection.

Many of the statewide and national public opinion surveys you read about in newspapers are conducted by contacting less than 2000 people. Tests prove that you would get the same results if you contacted 10 times that number, or more. It's just a statistical fact of life that a well-chosen small sample will give the same results as a much larger sample.

In local elections, to be on the safe side, work with about 10% of the registered voters.

The procedure is simple:

* First, decide what you want to know. Do you want to know **what** issues are important, **why** they are important, or both? Or, if you are trying to determine your standing with the voters, do you want to know how many will vote for you, or where you stand in relation to other candidates?

* Next, write a series of questions designed to extract the information you are seeking. It is important to take all bias out of questions: write them in a manner which does not prompt a specific answer, but gives voters an opportunity to express their feelings.

71

* Then organize your questions in a logical sequence. It is good to start with easy questions like, "Are you aware of such-and-such problem (or issue)?" From there go on to ask questions about the issue. You may want to ask the same question in different words as a method of verifying the opinions expressed. In that case, you would put different versions of the question in different parts of the survey.

* Now decide whom to call. One of the simplest methods is to select every 10th name on the voter registration list. This would give you 10% of the voting population if you could reach every person designated. However, the odds are that some people will not have listed telephones and others will not be available when you call. Therefore, you establish a system for dealing with this problem, like going to the 11th name if you can't reach the 10th name.

* Now all that remains is to get people to make the telephone calls. This requires finding people who are comfortable making calls to strangers and who will follow the script. It also means picking a time when most people are home, such as 6-9 p.m., Mondays through Thursdays. (Calling after 9 p.m. can irritate people; Friday evenings and weekends you'll discover a lot of people are not home.)

WHEN TO CONDUCT POLLS AND SURVEYS

If you are running for a major office such as County Board of Supervisors, District Attorney, Assessor, Sheriff, it can be extremely important to know what issues the public thinks are important and which way the voters lean on major issues.

You may also want to do a quick poll to determine in which areas you have name recognition and in which areas your name is relatively unknown. Or, if it appears that there may be several candidates in the race, you may want to do a poll to discover how you stand in relation to other potential candidates.

Voter interest in campaigns is usually low until the last few weeks. However, voter concerns about certain issues may be very high long before any candidates enter the picture. Thus, it can be to your advantage to conduct a survey six months or more before an election to identify key issues.

You can make good use of polls during a campaign with what are known as tracking polls. These are simple, short lists of questions designed to detect shifts in public opinion. Example: If you conducted a name recognition or popularity poll six months before the election, you would want to repeat it three months later and again three weeks before the election to see where you stand.

Tracking polls during a campaign--the last four to six weeks before the election--also serve to show you areas where you are doing well and areas where you must do more work.

PHONE BANKS

Phone banks serve one purpose: to identify supporters by name so you can call them on election day to remind them to vote.

As a by-product, phone banks also help to identify your strength, precinct by precinct. You also gain name recognition in the process and, on occasion, pick up additional campaign workers.

In a typical suburban campaign, one phone bank is used about three weeks before the election. However, it takes several weeks of planning and preparation, so someone should be assigned to the project about six weeks before election day.

These are the steps involved:

Step #1 - Order a voter list printout.

The County Clerk sells voter registration lists to candidates and their committees. At the time you file your nomination papers, order precinct sheets which list voters according to street addresses, precinct by precinct. You will use these in later precinct walking to identify houses where there are registered voters.

Allow time for the County Clerk to make the printout. This can be two weeks or more, depending upon the workload in the County Clerk's office.

Be prepared to pay for the printout when you pick it up. The cost is nominal. In 1981 the typical cost was 50¢ per 1,000 names. Thus, in a community with 10,000 voters, your cost will be $5.

Step #2 - Appoint a Phone Bank Chairman.

Select your Phone Bank Chairman as early as possible: someone who is good at organizing, can follow through with details, will work with minimum supervision, gets along well with volunteers.

Step #3 - List priority precincts.

The Steering Committee and Phone Bank Chairman should

work together to list all precincts in your area in priority order. The most important precincts are those which have the highest record of voter turnout. This you can discover by having someone check the County Clerk's records of recent elections.

The purpose in establishing a priority list for precincts is that, if you don't have enough volunteers to call all precincts, at least you can cover the most important ones.

Step #4 - Organize a Phone Bank Committee.

The Phone Bank Chairman's first job is to find volunteers to help prepare precinct lists, to add missing telephone numbers, to keep records and to make telephone calls. Remember, some volunteers don't like to make telephone calls, but they are happy to help with the paperwork. Get all the volunteers you can because there is a lot of detail work to do.

Step #5 - Up-date telephone listings.

Voters are not required to list telephone numbers when they register to vote. There is space for telephone numbers on the form, but only about half the voters list their numbers.

The first task of the volunteers is to go through the precinct sheets, using a telephone book or a reverse directory, to insert missing telephone numbers. Don't worry that your list will never be 100% correct. Some people have unlisted numbers, some have no telephones, some obtained their telephones after the directories were published.

Step #6 - Write instructions and a script.

Your telephone callers need instructions to make calls and to record information on printout sheets. Also, they do a better job if you give them a script to follow when they make calls.

Sample instructions and a script are at the end of this essay.

Your instructions should include a system for indicating how voters stand, such as:

* "S" - supporters.

* "O" - opposition.

* "U" - undecided.

* "X" - unaware of the election.

Step #7 - Set dates and times for making calls.

Two weeks before election day is ideal for making phone bank calls, if you have enough volunteers to do the job quickly. Otherwise, do it about three weeks before the election. The reason for waiting until later in the campaign is that voters will have had more time to see your campaign material.

The best days to call are Monday through Thursday because too many people are away Fridays and weekends.

The best time to call is 6-8:30 p.m. This catches most people at home and means fewer call-backs. In some communities it is acceptable to call as late as 9 p.m., but you run the danger of irritating people if you call any later.

To estimate the number of people you need to make calls and how many hours or days the project will take, work on the basis of 30 calls per hour per volunteer. This allows two minutes per call, which is ample to dial a number, get a voter on the phone, ask a few questions and make the appropriate notations on the call sheets.

At this rate, with each caller working 2½ hours an evening, you can reach about 150 voters. With 10 callers, you can reach 1500 people a night.

Be prepared to make some call-backs due to busy lines or people not answering telephones. Also, don't be surprised when you discover a fair number of wrong numbers and disconnected telephones.

Step #8 - Train volunteers.

You want volunteers who have pleasant voices, speak clearly and will follow instructions.

Get your volunteers together and go through the instructions and the script with each of them. Then let them practice on one another until they feel comfortable with the process.

Step #9 - Make the calls.

Complete the telephoning as quickly as possible once you start.

Volunteer callers get more done when they work as a group in a central location. This group arrangement also gives you the opportunity to provide a supervisor to answer difficult questions.

Some people will offer to make calls from their homes. This is fine if you can trust them to do the job. Unfortunately, there is a temptation when you are working alone to make a few calls and then stop to do other things and not complete the job on schedule.

Step #10 - Tally and analyze the results.

Count how many people were called, how many were reached, and the number of people who said they support you, oppose you, were undecided, or didn't know there was an election coming up.

You also want names of people who asked for more information or who volunteered to work in the campaign.

After the numbers are tallied, have volunteers go through the sheets and "highlight" the names of supporters, using felt pens (yellow is best) which are available in most stationery stores.

If you chart calls and responses, precinct by precinct, you can see immediately where you have the greatest strength and where you are weakest.

Step #11 - Use the results on election day.

Having identified your supporters by name, you are in a position to mount a get-out-the-vote effort on election day. This is a simple matter of having people go to the polling places about 4:30 p.m. to check off the names of supporters who have already voted so other people can call those who have not voted to remind them to vote. This process, like the Phone Bank, takes advance preparation, so an essay on the subject has been prepared for you.

INSTRUCTIONS FOR PHONE BANK CALLERS

Thank you for volunteering to help with the phone bank. This is an important project. It helps to pinpoint our supporters by name, plus building name recognition for (candidate's name) and, possibly, recruiting more volunteers.

Please follow these instructions:

1. Follow the script which is attached.

2. Call every household. Call only one person in each family. It's not always true, but families often vote for the same candidate.

3. Record results in pencil. To the right of the voter's name, write S for supporter, 0 for opposition, U for undecided and X if they are not familiar with (candidate's name) or don't know there is an election coming up. Write "more info" if they ask for additional information and "will work" if they volunteer to work.

4. Wrong numbers. When you get a wrong number, put a line through the number, but not the voter's name.

5. No answer. Let the phone ring 5 times. If no one answers, go on to the next call. After you have completed your assigned pages, go back and try the "no answers" a second or third time.

6. Keep conversations short. Remember, the purpose is to reach as many voters as possible. If people ask questions, offer to send them more information, then make a note on the call sheet.

7. Be polite at all times. No matter what people say when you call them, be polite. Remember, we still want their votes.

8. Speak clearly and loud enough, but don't shout.

(SAMPLE)

PHONE BANK CALLERS' SCRIPT

Please follow this script when making calls:

When the telephone is answered:

HELLO. IS THIS (name of voter)?

if it is not the voter, ask:

MAY I PLEASE SPEAK TO (name of voter)?

If asked why, or who you are, reply:

WE ARE CONDUCTING A SURVEY FOR THE (name of office) ELECTION.

When you get the voter on the line:

HELLO. I AM (your name), A VOLUNTEER WORKING FOR (name of candidate) WHO IS RUNNING FOR (name of office). WE ARE CONDUCTING A VOTER SURVEY WHICH TAKES LESS THAN A MINUTE TO COMPLETE.

ARE YOU AWARE OF THE ELECTION ON (date) FOR (name of office)?

(Do not record answer at this point)

FROM WHAT YOU KNOW OF THE CANDIDATES, WOULD YOU BE INCLINED TO VOTE FOR (name of candidate) IF THE ELECTION WERE HELD TODAY?

After you get a response:

THANK YOU VERY MUCH FOR YOUR TIME.

If people interrupt to ask questions, offer to send them information. If they offer to work in the campaign, make note of their names. If they hang up without answering questions, record an X for a response.

Organizing Invitational Events

Receptions, Luncheons, Dinners, Kickoffs

Invitational events are important to raise money, generate publicity, recruit campaign workers and create enthusiasm.

Events don't run themselves. They require planning, preparation and careful attention to a thousand and one details.

This essay is written primarily for people in charge of planning and managing invitational events.

In addition to suggestions offered here, the Appendix contains a set of checklists to help you with every step in the process.

Advice to candidates: Put the job of organizing and managing events into the hands of a very reliable person who has no other campaign responsibilities. You participate in the process of deciding the purpose, size and scope of an event; leave details to others.

PRELIMINARY DECISIONS

The Campaign Manager and Steering Committee must make a series of preliminary decisions before an event can be planned in detail:

* **Purpose:** fundraising, publicity, recruiting, other.

* **Audience:** contributors, campaign workers, other.

* **Timing:** weekday, weekend, midday, afternoon, evening.

* **Site:** public, private, indoors, outdoors, other.

* **Dress:** formal, informal, casual, costume.

* **Invitations:** RSVP or not, mail, phone, limited, unlimited.

* **Financing:** self-supporting, ticket sales, from campaign budget, outside hosts.

* **Food:** full meal, snacks, buffet, potluck, brown bag.

* **Service:** sit-down, catered, volunteers, buffet.

* **Beverages:** no-host, free, punch only, wine only, champagne, full bar, coffee, tea, milk, soft drinks.

* **Program:** background music, entertainment, speeches, VIP introductions, M.C.

* **Budget.**

ORGANIZATION

The event chairman should form a small committee of volunteers to plan the event, then appoint chairmen for separate functions: invitations, program, decorations, food, ticket sales, hospitality, publicity, advertising, even cleanup after the event.

The checklists and the Appendix will give you an idea of how to combine functions.

PLANNING

The event chairman and planning group can complete the planning job faster and more efficiently by taking it in four steps:

Step 1. - Establish a written schedule.

Work backwards from the date of the event. Set dates when each action must be started and completed.

Example: (An Oct. 2 event)

Sept. 28 - Complete RSVP calls.

Sept. 23 - Start RSVP follow-up calls.

Sept. 11 - Invitations in the mail.

Sept. 9 - Finish addressing invitations.

Sept. 3 - Start addressing invitations.

Sept. 2 - Complete invitation list.

Aug. 28 - Start compiling invitation list.

Step 2. - Assign responsibilities.

Assign responsibility for every function. As an example, one person in charge of compiling the invitation list, another for getting invitations printed, a third person for getting volunteers to address invitations, a fourth for follow-up telephone calls.

Step 3. - Create a record system.

Set up files to keep track of everything involved in the event from the guest list, to RSVP responses, to the menu and names and telephone numbers of volunteers working on the project. Also set up financial records with the help of the campaign Treasurer.

Step 4. - Plan for contingencies.

Avoid headaches by planning in advance to deal with a variety of contingencies. This is a job for the event planning group. All that needs to be done is to ask a series of "what if" questions, then decide what to do. For instance, if an outdoor event is planned, what if it rains? Will the event be cancelled, postponed, moved to another location, or what?

GENERAL HINTS

1. Plan events which are appropriate to your community and your type of campaign. Example: formal dress events at a high cost per guest are not approrpriate for low-budget district campaigns.

2. Campaign kickoff events in most local campaigns work best on weekends in mid-afternoon. This is not necessarily the best time for the news media, but check with editors about how they want to cover events.

3. Look for sites where you will not be charged a rental fee; otherwise, look for a place with a low charge.

4. Keep costs down. Use volunteers wherever possible to prepare and serve food, tend bar, make decorations, provide background music and entertainment.

5. At fundraisers, revenue is more important than the number of people who attend.

6. At publicity events, numbers of people attending are most important.

7. People invited to most political events expect to make contributions. Make it easy, by having bowls, boxes or other containers readily available.

8. Keep speech-making to a minimum! Have the M.C. introduce distinguished guests, particularly elected officials and former elected officials. But do not invite them to speak. Whoever introduces the candidate should

do it in two minutes or less and the candidate should limit his or her comments to five minutes saying, in effect, "This is what I intend to do, if elected, and I need all the help I can get."

9. A candidate should circulate constantly, meeting everyone attending the event.

10. Have campaign materials readily available at the reception desk and elsewhere in the room.

11. Use a sign-in system so you have the name, address and telephone number of every person who attends.

12. At a kick-off or reception, pick a time midway through the event to begin the program. Have one person designated to decide when that time arrives and start with the introduction of VIPs.

13. At stand-up events, most guests will remain an hour or a little more. For a reception beginning at 3 p.m., you can anticipate the largest crowd about 4:30.

14. Think carefully before deciding to serve hard liquor. It's expensive and it isn't necessary: champagne, wine and punch are satisfactory. But always have non-alcoholic beverages available.

15. Invitations: Begin your list with people who are important politically. Use written invitations (printed or hand-written), mailed first class to home addresses. Include as many people as possible on the list, even when you know they will not attend; they are flattered by being invited and might get angry if they are not.

16. Invitation responses: Put RSVP and a telephone number (or several) on invitations.

    Set up a system for keeping track of responses. A telephone answering machine works well if you cannot have someone available at the listed telephone numbers day and night. Be sure the message on the machine identifies the campaign committee.

    Prepare to make follow-up telephone calls to people who do not respond by whatever date you have set as a cut-off.

17. Background music is nice in a large room; be sure it is not too loud; people like to mix and talk.

18. Have enough chairs for 15-20% of your guests.

19. Try to have a public address system, even for a small event. Be sure to test it before the event starts.

20. Designate a time for each event to end and have someone bring it to a close. One way is to remove the food and drink.

21. Have a committee especially for clean-up after the event--that day or the following day.

22. Arrange to have pictures taken during the event, primarily for your own use. They make nice mementos for volunteers. They also make good material for bulletin boards, campaign albums, brochures, advertising and publicity.

23. Publicity: Distribute a news release so it can be published about a week before the event.

   Here are a few additional suggestions about publicity.

   In the lead paragraph, include the name of the candidate, nature of the event, location, date and time.

   If the public is invited, say so; otherwise don't.

   Mention names of volunteers responsible for planning the event. They appreciate the recognition.

   If the media are invited, say so in a note at the bottom of the release; include the time the candidate is scheduled to make comments. This helps editors.

   Treat the news-gathering side of the media separately from executives. Reporters and photographers are there to do a job; executives are present to enjoy themselves.

   Send releases to all publications and radio and TV stations which reach your community, not just to one or two leading publications.

24. Handling the media: Assign one person to watch for reporters and photographers and to take care of their needs. Don't charge them for meals.

News & Publicity Tips

This essay is for everyone in a campaign who deals with news and publicity.

The secret for getting cooperation from the news media (newspapers, TV, radio) is to learn:

...what makes news.

...which news media are interested.

...who makes decisions.

...what editors and reporters want.

...how to meet deadlines.

...how to create news.

...how to use pictures.

WHAT MAKES NEWS

Forget the notion that news or publicity is "free advertising." It isn't. You pay for advertising and control what it says. You can't control news.

Editors define news as: action, change, controversy.

Not all "news" qualifies for use in local newspapers or on local television and radio stations. It must interest a substantial number of people in the area.

WHICH MEDIA ARE INTERESTED

News media interest in local campaigns depends upon the area they cover. Regional TV and radio stations cover large areas and cannot afford to cover local elections. Whatever coverage they give is limited to big city races. Nevertheless, check with TV and radio news directors before giving up on the broadcast media.

Big city newspapers have the same problem. The exception is when a metropolitan newspaper has regional sections. Then they will give some coverage to major local races, like county Board of Supervisors.

When you get away from the large population centers, some TV and radio stations cover campaigns in their areas.

In some areas, cable TV stations have local news shows or give time to candidates.

Local daily and weekly newspapers cover local campaigns in direct proportion to what editors perceive as the degree of public interest in the races. This is why City Council campaigns receive more attention than Fire Board or Water Board races.

Another class of publications serves special audiences: senior citizens, retired people, business and professional groups and affinity groups (people with common interests). In some areas, these can be very important outlets.

WHO MAKES DECISIONS

The decision-making process varies with the size and nature of the news organization.

TV and radio: news directors decide which campaigns to cover; assignment editors select stories; any staff reporter may be assigned to cover a story. TV and radio stations rarely endorse candidates, except in big city major races.

Daily newspapers: publishers or editors, or an editorial group, decide which candidates to endorse; city editors decide stories to cover and publicity materials to use; political editors track campaigns and sometimes have the final word on which campaign stories and publicity materials to use; various reporters are assigned to individual events. On papers with reporters assigned to "beats" (like City Hall or Education), it is important to get to know those who cover the office you are seeking.

Weekly newspapers: publishers and editors usually decide jointly which candidate to endorse; editors decide stories to cover, assign reporters and sometimes cover stories themselves. Often, one reporter covers all campaigns in a given election.

Special purpose publications: the editors usually do everything.

WHAT EDITORS AND REPORTERS WANT

Editors want anything of interest to their viewers, listeners or readers. They want it immediately, while it is news, not days later when the news value is gone.

They want facts <u>they</u> consider important, not just your version. Thus, you must be prepared to answer questions.

Local newspaper editors are interested in people in the

community. This is why they print names of people who organize events or prominent people who endorse candidates.

DEADLINES

All news media operate on firm deadlines. Don't risk losing good stories by missing deadlines.

Deadlines vary, so you should contact broadcasters and editors early in the campaign to make sure you know their deadlines. Here are examples:

* **Weekly papers:** Papers published Wednesdays usually have Monday news deadlines. The feature section--and sometimes this is where political campaign news appears--often has a Friday deadline. Letters to the Editor deadlines are Thursdays or Fridays. News photo deadline may be Fridays or Mondays; feature pictures, Thursdays or Fridays.

* **Morning Dailies:** The news deadline is usually about 8 p.m. the night before. Feature stories are earlier. The news photo deadline is usually a few hours earlier than the news deadline. Letters to the Editors are published several days after they are received.

* **Afternoon Dailies:** The news deadline is about 11 a.m. the day of publication. Feature story deadlines are a day or more earlier. Letters to the Editors appear several days after they are received. The news photo deadline is usually about an hour before the news deadline.

* **Special purpose publications:** Deadlines vary with publications, usually earlier than for weekly newspapers.

* **TV:** Each station has its own series of deadlines. Usually the last filming is completed at least two hours before air time.

* **Radio:** Radio stations have a series of deadlines, one for each news program. Live interviews (including telephone) can be done up to an hour before air time. Written news releases usually have a deadline several hours before air time.

HOW TO CREATE NEWS

Learn to think like an editor.
Look for stories that interest large numbers of people. Ask

yourself, "Who cares?" If the answer is that many people care, you have a story; if only a handful care, you don't.

Look for ways to make routine stories interesting or unusual: the first, the biggest, the smallest--anything different or unusual.

Timing can decide what makes news. For example, a Thursday event has minimum news value for a weekly paper published on Wednesday. A Saturday afternoon event loses some news value for newspapers with no Sunday editions. Staging any event which conflicts with a more important news event can ruin a good story.

There are things which make news in any campaign:

* Candidacy announcements.

* Filing nomination papers.

* Appointment of the Campaign Committee Chairman.

* Appointments of other key people.

* Kick-off events.

* Announcements of fundraising events.

* Schedules of coffees and other public appearances.

* Statements made at public events.

* Charges leveled at other candidates.

* Responses to charges.

* Reactions to major news events, such as federal and state decisions concerning cities, in a City Council race.

* Endorsements by organizations.

* Endorsements by prominent people.

HANDLING INTERVIEWS

Remember just one rule: if you don't want it in print or on the air, don't say it.

It is vitally important to know how to handle news interviews. Do it right and you look good; do it wrong, you look stupid.

There are three ways to make interviews work in your favor:

1.   Before an interview, try to anticipate the questions; then frame answers in your mind.

2. Listen carefully to questions; answer what you are asked. Don't drift off into other subjects.

3. Answer questions clearly, concisely and truthfully. Don't be evasive.

THE USE OF PICTURES

Provide all publications in your area with a photograph (face) at the beginning of a campaign. Be prepared to have editors ask you to pose for a picture. Many prefer to use their own.

Few newspapers will use your pictures of events, except when they agree in advance to do so. They prefer to take their own.

Picture policies vary with publications. Check with editors.

Television is essentially a picture medium: stories with something to photograph--people doing things. The last thing they want--but use if necessary--is a "talking head."

Advertising

Advertising is any kind of paid message: posters, signs, fliers, direct mail, paid space in newspapers, radio and television commercials, even the Candidate's Statement of Qualifications in the voter pamphlet.

Advertising serves many purposes, among them:

* To build name recognition.

* To maintain public awareness of the candidate's name.

* To raise money.

* To promote events.

* To discuss and debate issues.

* To appeal for votes.

Because campaign budgets are always limited and all forms of advertising are expensive, it is important that you learn how to get the most for your money: first, by being cost-effective when you select materials and outlets; second, by communicating effectively.

BE COST-EFFECTIVE

Cost-effectiveness can be measured by what you pay to reach each voter with a messge. But you can't stop there. You must also consider the effectiveness of one kind of advertising compared to others.

Here's a simple example. Suppose a full page ad in the local newspaper costs $600 and the paper is delivered to 10,000 homes. Assuming there are 2.5 residents per home, you reach 25,000 people for $600. That's 2.4¢ per reader (dividing the cost by the number of readers).

However, not all readers are voters. Only about 60% of the population is registered to vote and only about 30% of those registered show up at the polls in most local elections. Thus, you take 60% of 25,000 readers and that gives you 15,000 eligible voters. Divide that number into the cost of the ad and your cost almost doubles (4¢ per voter).

Now life gets complicated. Your $600 ad appears in only one issue of the paper. Not every reader sees it and, of those who do, you don't know how many will remember it. Thus, you must consider whether the $600 would be better spent for a large sign along a well-travelled highway, seen by motorists for five or six weeks, or $600 worth of bumper stickers, or 4,000 fliers mailed to known supporters.

The thought may also occur to you that something less than a full-page ad might be more cost-effective. You are right. You can dominate a newspaper page with a half-page ad, or be effective with one even smaller if it is designed properly.

The nature of your community sometimes determines what is cost-effective. For example, if there are only a few main thoroughfares leading into and out of the community, signs and posters along roadways can be very effective. Conversely, if there are too many main roads, the cost per sign and poster coverage becomes prohibitive.

Residents of some communities have an intense dislike of campaign signs. Thus, even though they might be seen by a lot of voters, they could have a negative effect on your campaign.

The same might be true of bumper stickers and lawn signs.

Probably the most cost-effective advertising is door-to-door delivery by volunteers of a good campaign brochure. All you pay is the cost of printing; then deliver only to homes of registered voters.

NEWSPAPER ADVERTISING

Newspaper advertising plays a prominent role because it is effective for mass communications.

Normally you deal with four kinds of publications:

1. Area or regional newspapers, some of which have local editions in which you can buy advertising.

2. Local newspapers covering all or parts of your voting area.

3. "Shoppers" mailed or delivered free to all households in your area.

4.   Special interest publications: senior citizen newspapers, high school and college newspapers, athletic event programs, any publication which reaches a limited group.

It is obvious that the cost per voter reached is an important consideration.   But not always.   One newspaper might reach substantially more voters than another paper costing less per reader.

Pay particular attention to the special interest publications. A good example is senior citizen newspapers.   Senior citizens have a much better voting record than any other age group.   Therefore, an ad in one of their publications reaches a higher percentage of people who actually vote than an ad in a general circulation newspaper.   Or an ad in the high school Homecoming Game program can reach a large number of young voters and parents.

ADVERTISING SIZES

There are no "rules" about what size ads are most effective but there are several things to consider:

* **Full-page ads** give you more space for a message or a list of people endorsing you.

* **Less-than-full-page ads** can dominate a page if they are laid out properly.   Let ad managers help.

* **Front page boxes,** usually one column wide and three or four inches high, get attention.   However, you pay a stiff premium; sometimes double the cost of space inside.

* **Classified ads** can be very effective to maintain name awareness or to deliver one-sentence messages.

TIMING YOUR ADVERTISING

Remember, most voters don't pay much attention to campaigns until the last few weeks.   That's when you concentrate your major effort.

If you plan a series of ads--at least three--use the first to establish your qualifications: honors, awards, education, organization affiliations, record of community involvement.

Use the second ad, or group, to discuss issues.

The final ad, or ads, should appear on the Friday, Saturday

91

or Monday before the Tuesday election. This is the time to appeal for votes. Publish names of people and organizations who endorse you, or divide the ad into two parts, one for names, the other to repeat qualifications and positions on issues.

REQUIRED CONTENTS

California (FPPC) laws require that:

1. Political advertisements be identified with "Paid Political Advertisement" in type at least one-half the size of the type in the advertisement, or 10-point Roman type, whichever is larger.

   These words must be set apart from any other part of the ad. Newspapers often put the words above the main body of the ad, without charging for the space.

2. The name and the address of the campaign committee must be printed within each ad, with the name of the Chairman or Treasurer and the committee Identification Number (issued by the California Secretary of State).

3. When a simulated ballot or sample ballot is used in an ad (or elsewhere in the campaign), it must also have a notice to voters in a separate box with borders. The type in the box must be at least half the size of the type in the ad or in 10-point Roman type, whichever is larger. The notice must read as follows:

NOTICE TO VOTERS
(Required by Law)

This is not an official ballot or an official sample ballot prepared by the county clerk, registrar of voters, or the Secretary of State.

This is an unofficial, marked ballot prepared by

_____

(insert name and address of the person or organization responsible for preparation thereof.)

Further, no official seal or insignia of any public entity (government agency or office) can be used in ads or other campaign materials.

HINTS FOR LAYOUTS AND CONTENT

Ads must capture readers' attention to be effective. That's done with good design, called layout--the size and placement of pictures, headlines and blocks of copy.

You hold readers' attention by making type large enough to read easily and wording easy to understand.

Pictures are always eye-catchers. Use your photograph (face) and place it near the top of the ad so you appear to be looking "into" the ad.

One-word and two-word headlines in large type capture attention. Action verbs work best: **BEWARE!...END WASTE!...YOU DECIDE!**

People won't read long, complicated sentences. Nor long paragraphs. Condense what you have to say into very few words.

A coupon at the bottom of an ad can be useful to get endorsements and to recruit campaign workers. Provide space for people to print their names, addresses and telephone numbers. Ask for signatures. Don't forget to give an address where coupons can be mailed and a telephone number where people can get information.

PREPARATION FOR PUBLICATION

The final step is to deliver your materials to the advertising department, write an insertion order and pay for the ad.

Advertising departments give customers all kinds of help without charge: suggestions for the layout, type sizes and type faces; provide decorations and illustrations; set the type, paste up the ad and give you a proof to read.

Ad deadlines are earlier than news deadlines. Be sure to check with the ad department well in advance so you have time to proofread your ad.

You can ask to have your ad published in a particular place in the newspaper. Most papers will do their best to accommodate you, but they will not guarantee position.

RADIO AND TELEVISION ADVERTISING

We have said little about radio and television advertising, and for good reason: it's too expensive in most local campaigns. You would be paying to reach an audience where 90% of the people are not eligible to vote for you.

There are always exceptions, of coure. If you are in an area which has local radio or television stations and the rates are reasonable, advertising might be worth the investment.

"Get-Out-The-Vote" Campaigns

Local elections can be won or lost by a mere handful of votes: 10 or less can make the difference.

A simple "get-out-the-vote" campaign on election day is one way to make sure that your known supporters get out and vote.

Briefly, this is how it works: about 4 p.m., volunteers go to polling places and check off the names of known supporters who have voted. Another group then calls supporters who have <u>not</u> voted to remind them to vote. They also offer rides to the polls which are provided by a third group of volunteers.

Sometimes you repeat the process about 6 p.m. so that the final calls are made about an hour before the polls close.

PREPARATION

Preparation must begin weeks in advance so you have the materials and volunteers available to complete the poll-checking and telephoning in less than four hours. You have only one shot at these last-minute votes, so you have to do it right.

Step #1 – Appoint a chairman
Look for a person who is well-organized and has no other responsibilities the last weeks of the campaign.

Step #2 – Recruit volunteers
You need people to: check names at polling places; call supporters who have not voted; drive voters to polls and home again.

Step #3 – Mark the voter sheets
Use the voter sheets from the earlier Phone Bank which lists voters by street address, by precinct. Have volunteers mark the names of supporters with yellow "highlight" felt pens, including:

* Voters identified during the Phone Bank.

* Names picked up during door-to-door campaigning.

* People who signed endorsement cards.

* Supporters picked up at coffees.

* Names from sign-in sheets from events.

* Financial contributors and campaign committee members.

Remember, mark only known supporters: sure votes!

Step #4 - Write instructions for volunteers.
Provide written instructions for all three functions. Samples are provided at the end of this essay.

Step #5 - Locate sites for making calls.
With only about three hours to call supporters, you need people on telephones at several sites in order to get the job done. Even if you have a campaign headquarters, you may not have enough telephone lines, so people will have to make calls from homes.

Locate more sites than you need, to be safe. Then make a list of the sites, with addresses and telephone numbers.

Establish one site or telephone exclusively for in-coming calls from poll-checkers to reach the "get-out-the-vote" chairman.

Step #6 - Make a work schedule and phone list.
Prepare a written schedule, showing which volunteers check what polling places, and when. Assign people in teams, one person to check off names on the official lists of people who have voted; the other person to check your precinct sheets.

Assign teams to check at 4:30 p.m. and 6-6:30.

Make a chart, listing precincts in numerical order, so you can check off precincts as poll-checkers call in; make a check mark in the second column when calls to voters have been completed.

Make a list of polling places, with addresses and the precincts they include. Use this to direct people to their jobs. Give poll-checkers slips of paper with their precinct addresses.

Step #7 - Provide supplies and rides for volunteers.
Poll-checkers and telephone-callers need pencils--several each. They also need rulers to read across lines on precinct sheets. Also, be nice, provide coffee and soft drinks at the headquarters.

Be sure volunteers have transportation to work sites and back.

ELECTION DAY

1.   Assemble volunteers.
Have all volunteers meet at one location at 4 p.m. for assignments and final instructions. Make sure they know their jobs.

2. Dispatch poll-checkers.

Start with high priority precincts and work your way down until you run out of volunteers.

3. Dispatch remaining volunteers.

Send telephone-callers and drivers to their respective sites. Ask extra volunteers to remain at the headquarters.

4. Start checking precincts about 4:30 p.m.

Election officials start posting their voter sheets about 4:00 p.m. Your poll-checkers should start work as soon as the official sheets are posted.

Have them call in or bring their sheets in as they complete each precinct. Make sure that all precinct sheets are in the hands of the project chairman before the end of the day.

5. Assign callers.

Assign volunteers to call supporters who have not voted. Give each caller a page or two at a time.

Don't worry about getting precinct sheets mixed up; you can assemble them later.

Have the telephone-callers set aside sheets with names of people who have not voted and whose phones don't answer. Reassign these sheets for follow-up calls before the polls close.

6. Assign Drivers.

Assign drivers to take voters to the polls and home again as requests for rides are received.

7. Keep records up to date.

Be sure to check off each precinct as the poll-checkers call in so you know which precincts have been covered.

8. Check precincts a second time.

Do it again about 6:30 to reach people who were late returning from work or shopping.

9. Gather the precinct sheets.

The last act is to gather all the precinct sheets. You or someone else will want them for the next campaign.

Now go to the Victory Party.

(SAMPLE)

"GET-OUT-THE-VOTE"

POLL-CHECKER INSTRUCTIONS

1. You have been given a list of voters in one precinct and the address of the polling place for that precinct. <u>Note: names of our supporters are marked on your sheets.</u>

2. Go to the polling place about 4 p.m. Look for the voter list. It should be posted outside the voting room. Election officials are required to post this list, beginning about 4 p.m. Names of people who have voted are checked off. Officials update lists about once an hour.

3. If a list is not posted, ask one of the election officials when it will be available. Do not leave the area; wait for the list to be posted.

4. One person should read names off the official list while the other member of your team checks off names on our voter sheets. Check off only people who have voted.

5. When you finish checking a precinct, call in or deliver your sheets to (address) so we can start calling people who have <u>not</u> voted. The earlier you call, the earlier we can start making phone calls.

6. If you are assigned to check the same polling places a second time, hang on to your voter list. Otherwise turn it in when you complete checking the first time.

7. <u>Be sure that all voter sheets are turned in before you go home!!!</u>

(SAMPLE)

"GET-OUT-THE-VOTE"

TELEPHONE-CALLER INSTRUCTIONS

1. You have been given voter lists with names of our supporters marked. The names of people who have already voted today are also marked.

2. Call only supporters who have not yet voted.

3. Try to get the voter on the line; if necessary, leave a message: the same message you give to voters.

4. When you call, identify yourself by name and the campaign name and say:

   "I NOTICE THAT YOU HAVEN'T VOTED YET. WE NEED YOUR VOTE, SO I HOPE YOU CAN GET TO THE POLLS BEFORE THEY CLOSE AT 8:00 P.M. IF YOU NEED A RIDE, WE CAN ARRANGE TO TAKE YOU TO THE POLLS AND HOME AGAIN. THANK YOU VERY MUCH."

5. Keep conversation to a minimum so you can reach as many people as possible in the short time available.

6. Check off voter names after you make contact.

7. When people request rides, give their names to (name of person dispatching drivers).

8. If there is no answer, try again after you have gone through your sheets. If there is still no answer, give your sheet to (name).

9. People might ask how you know they have not voted. Tell them that election officials are required to post the voter list and we have people checking to make sure that all our supporters get out and vote today.

(SAMPLE)

"GET-OUT-THE-VOTE"

VOLUNTEER DRIVER INSTRUCTIONS

1. You have been given a list of precincts and polling places, with a map.

2. You will be given names and addresses of people requesting rides to and from the polls. These are known supporters--we hope!

3. When you arrive at an address, identify yourself by name; say you are a volunteer for (name of candidate) here to provide a ride to the polling place and back.

4. You may be asked about (the candidate) during the ride. You should know enough by now to answer any reasonable questions.

5. You are permitted to help your passenger into the voting area, but you cannot go into the voting booth.

6. Campaigning is forbidden within 100 feet of a polling place. If you have campaign signs or stickers on your vehicle, please park at least 150 feet from the polling place to avoid criticism.

7. When you have delivered a passenger to his or her residence, please call (telephone number) for your next assignment. It is not necessary to return to the headquarters as long as we know where to reach you.

Recall Campaigns

Moves to recall local elected officials occur with enough frequency to focus attention on the subject briefly.

You could find yourself on either side of a recall move:

...as the target, or friend of the official fighting the recall action.

...or as part of the group sponsoring the recall.

In either case, there are things you should know about the process.

In California, the process is relatively simple:

* Elected officials cannot be recalled during the first 90 days or last six months of a term.

* Office-holders must be served written notice of intention by the recall sponsors and be given an opportunity to respond before petitions are printed.

* Sponsors must publish the notice of intention and a statement of grounds for their action in a local newspaper of general circulation.

* Petitions to put the question on the ballot must contain both the statement of grounds and the elected official's response, if any.

* Registered voters must sign petitions. The number varies according to the number of voters in the area and the public office involved.

* In some instances (certain offices), a candidate must be on the ballot to replace the person being recalled.

* A simple majority of those voting in the recall election decides the issue.

Specific requirements for a recall election are in the California Elections Code and also are available from any County Clerk.

People are often tempted to try to recall officials who are unpopular at the moment. But it isn't all that easy. A great many voters dislike the process, except when gross abuse of public office is involved or, as some say, "you got caught with your hand in the cookie jar."

However, in spite of this feeling, recall movements are launched every year and a fair number succeed.

Recalls seem to have the best chance of succeeding when highly emotional local issues are involved and elected officials act contrary to prevailing public wishes. As an example, three members of one City Council--the majority--were recalled in one election. At issue were decisions affecting growth, conservation and ecology. Citizens disliked several decisions permitting new developments, commercial and residential. One reason the recall succeeded, according to those involved in it, was that the City Council decisions had affected several neighborhoods, giving the recall sponsors a broad base of support from the outset.

Once a recall qualifies for the ballot, the campaign on both sides is much like any election campaign: you must reach and persuade enough voters to prevail; you need organization, money, a plan and volunteers.

Both sides in a recall election begin with certain advantages. If you are sponsoring the action, you have a ready-made constituency among voters who signed the petitions. If you are on the defense, you can play on the public dislike of the recall process and build a coalition which includes people who, normally, would not be on your side.

Remember, if you plan a recall move, the taxpayers pay the cost of the election--whatever city, county or special district which is involved. If you don't have a good case, you not only lose the election, you harm your cause by creating an added expense for the taxpayers.

SAMPLE STATEMENTS OF QUALIFICATIONS

STATEMENT OF CANDIDATE FOR MEMBER, GOVERNING BOARD
MARIN COMMUNITY COLLEGE DISTRICT

JOSEPH E. DOHERTY
AGE: 40

Occupation: Incumbent

Education and Qualifications: I have lived and worked in Marin for 14 years with my wife, Elizabeth, and daughters, Rachel and Sarah. I am a homeowner in Novato. I am a juvenile probation officer in Marin County.

I have an A.B. in philosophy from St. Mary's, graduate work in theology, and an M.A. in counseling.

As an eight year member of the Board of Trustees my goals have been to:

- keep our Community Colleges open to all Marin residents;

- maintain academic excellence;

- be fiscally responsible to the taxpayers.

My leadership on the Board has helped to reduce the construction and facilities budget by 50%, aided the coordination of county-wide adult education, the opening of a Small Business Institute, and the restructuring of personnel policies and procedures.

The challenge of the eighties will be:

- continued academic excellence in the face of declining income;

- maintaining local control in spite of increased state regulations.

With two Board members retiring, stability is important. Thus, my re-election on November 3rd, will insure continuity of academic excellence, fiscal responsibility and the stable governance of **your** community colleges.

s/Joseph E. Doherty

STATEMENT OF CANDIDATE FOR DIRECTOR
NORTH MARIN COUNTY WATER DISTRICT

PATRICK L. SIMPKINS
AGE: 40

Occupation: Tax Consultant

Education and Qualifications: I have 17 years experience in taxes and accounting. President-elect of the Ignacio Rotary Club (and charter member). Trustee and treasurer of the Shoreline Trust for Educational Program Services (Steps). Member of the steering committee for the Environmental Action Committee of West Marin. Treasurer of the West Marin Lion's Club. Past Chairman of the Shoreline Unified School District's Ad Hoc Committee on the budget. My wife, Dian, and I are actively involved in 4-H programs and Little League. I own my own tax consulting business in Novato.

B.A. Degree in Accounting and M.A. Degree in History.

I BELIEVE:

★ The water district needs a member with a strong business background.

★ That the business of a water district is to provide clean, safe water to its consumers in the most economical manner possible. As a director, I will strive to implement this philosophy.

★ That North Marin Water District board members have no right to make the public pay for dental care for directors and their families nor to participate in the district's retirement plan.

I plan to challenge these policies if elected.

I ask for your vote on November 3rd.

s/Patrick L. Simpkins

SAMPLE PLEDGE/ENDORSEMENT/VOLUNTEER CARDS

COMMITTEE TO ELECT JOHN DOE
Box 252, Anytown CA 99999
Ed Smiles, Chairman * Roger Cash, Treasurer

I WANT TO HELP ELECT JOHN DOE TO THE ANYTOWN CITY
COUNCIL. I WILL:

___ Serve on a Committee	___ Distribute literature
___ Make phone calls	___ Write letters
___ Work at Headquarters	___ Type/Address letters
___ Put up signs	___ Host a coffee
___ Contribute money $_____	___ Help raise money

PLEASE PRINT: NAME_____

ADDRESS_____

PHONE: (HOME)_____(OFFICE)_____

SIGNATURE:_____

I SUPPORT JOSEPH E. DOHERTY FOR THE COLLEGE BOARD

NAME _____ PHONE _____

ADDRESS _____
(please print)

I WILL HELP BY DOING: ☐ MAILING OF POSTCARDS
    ☐ A FUNCTION AT MY HOME
    ☐ ADDRESSING AND/OR TYPING

I AM WILLING TO MAKE A FINANCIAL CONTRIBUTION ☐

YOU MAY USE MY NAME _____
(signature)

(SAMPLE) "DEAR FRIEND" CARD CONTROL SHEET

(For use with people taking cards to address and sign.)

Name	Address	Phone #	# Cards Taken	Date Deliv'd	Date Returned	# Cards Returned

SAMPLE BUDGETS

(City Council election; 25,000 registered voters.)

	LOW	HIGH
STARTUP COSTS:		
Statement of Qualifications	237.50	237.50
Precinct lists and map	16.50	16.50
Mailing labels	.--	270.00
Postal permit plus 3rd Class permit	80.00	80.00
City sign deposit/fee	30.00	30.00
CAMPAIGN MATERIALS:		
Pledge/Endorsement/Vol. cards (2500)	100.00	.--
Pledge/Endorsement/Vol. cards (5000)	.--	150.00
Brochure (12,500)	.--	1500.00
Flyers (20,000)	250.00	250.00
Dear Friend cards (5,000)	200.00	200.00
Posters (200)	.--	300.00
Signs (6)	.--	540.00
Bumper stickers (1,000)	.--	200.00
POSTAGE:		
Dear Friend cards (@ 10.4¢)	520.00	520.00
Brochures (@ 10.4¢)	.--	65.00
NEWSPAPER ADS:		
Half-page ad(s) @ $500.00	500.00	1500.00
Small ads @ $50.00	150.00	150.00
Front page box	.--	65.00
KICKOFF PARTY:		
Invitations, printed (500)	70.00	70.00
Postage, 1st class (20¢)	100.00	100.00
Wine/cheese/crackers/glasses	150.00	.--
Wine/coffee/soft drinks	.--	200.00
Building/room rental	.--	125.00
Catering	.--	300.00
MISCELLANEOUS (Xerox, pens, name tags)	50.00	100.00
CAMPAIGN TOTAL	**$2454.00**	**$8204.00**

SAMPLE CAMPAIGN SCHEDULE

City Council Election, April 6, 1982

These are typical dates for most major actions and decisions in a City Council campaign, depending upon people and money available and the intensity of the race.

Only the dates marked with an asterisk (*) are firm legal dates. These concern FPPC reports and filing dates.

In campaigns for county offices, such as Board of Supervisors, Sheriff, D.A., Assessor, etc., E-Day is the June Primary. In this kind of campaign, you would add more mailers to the schedule, perhaps conduct a voter opinion survey and the organizing process would begin as early as E-300.

*E+65	- Final FPPC report due (covers E-17 thru E+58).
E+1-5	- Take down signs and posters; get deposit refund from city/county Public Works Dept.
E-DAY	- 6-8 a.m. and 4-6 p.m., human billboards (people with placards) along main commuter routes.
	- 4-7:30 p.m., Get-Out-The-Vote campaign.
	- 9 p.m. Victory Party.
E-1, 3,4	- Final ads appear in daily papers--at least one with names of endorsers.
E-2,3	- Auto caravans thru residential and shopping areas.
E-6	- Final ads appear in weekly papers, at least one with names of endorsers.
	- Mail "Dear Friend" cards, if using 1st Class mail.
E-7	- Mail "last-minute" flyer, if necessary.
	- Submit ads to appear in dailypapers E-1,3,4.
E-10	- Mail "Dear Friend" cards, if using bulk 3rd class.
E-11	- Submit final ads for weekly papers.
*E-12	- FPPC report due (covering E-44 thru E-17).
E-12	- Final date for collecting endorsements to use in ads.

E-13   - Ad appears in weekly papers (cover issues).

E-14   - Put up remaining signs and posters, if any.

E-15   - Final date for collecting signed "Dear Friend" cards.

E-20   - Ad appears in weekly papers (cover qualifications).

       - Ad in daily papers (optional).

E-21   - Tracking poll to see where candidate stands.

E-28   - Conduct Phone Bank (for names of supporters).

E-30   - Distribute "Dear Friend" cards, with instructions.

E-35   - Mail major brochure to voter households (bulk rate).

*E-40 - FPPC report (from campaign beginning thru E-45).

E-41   - Start precinct walking and shopping center walking.

E-43   - (Sat. or Sun.) Major kickoff event, designed for publicity
or 44   but including fundraising.

E-59   - Fundraising event for major donors.

E-60   - First signs go up.

       - Start coffee schedule.

       - Begin endorsement drive.

       - Begin planning Phone Bank.

E-69   - Get sign permits from city/county Public Work Dept.

*E-70 - Extended filing deadline for non-incumbents, if any
         incumbent failed to file by E-75.

*E-75 - Filing deadline.

       - File nomination papers with sponsor signatures.

       - Submit and pay for Statement of Qualifications.

       - Issue news releases or have news conference.

       - Order precinct sheets, mailing labels, precinct maps from
         County Clerk.

E-89   - Register Campaign Committee with Secretary of State.

E-80   - Start printing campaign materials (brochure, etc.)

*E-90   - Filing period opens.

        - Start designing campaign materials.

        - Begin fundraising for early money needed.

E-107   - Print Pledge Cards and Candidate Fact Sheet for Fundraising needs.

E-108   - Open bank account.

E-110   - Complete draft campaign plan, strategy, budget.

E-130   - Form Organizing Committee.

        - Start assembling lists of contributors, supporters.

        - Decide type/size Campaign Committee, general strategy; estimate campaign costs.

E-150   - Decide to run after talking to family and friends, estimating support, considering requirements of campaigning and serving in office.

109

PART III

APPENDIX

CHECKLISTS

NOTES

GETTING ORGANIZED

The Candidate's First Steps

___ Requirements of the elective office are clear.

___ Time available to serve in office, if elected.

___ Time available to campaign properly.

___ No personal or business problems to interfere.

___ Family understands and approves plan to run for office.

___ Name recognition: High ___ Fair ___ Low ___

___ List bases of support in community.

___ List sources of financial support.

___ Identify major issues.

___ Decide positions on issues.

___ Decide general campaign strategy.

___ Estimate campaign cost.

___ Write personal fact sheet: qualifications, positions.

___ Outline plan and schedule for getting organized.

___ Discuss plans with friends.

___ Form Organizing Committee.

NOTES _____

_____

_____

_____

GETTING ORGANIZED

Candidate & Organizing Committee Actions
Leading to Formation of Campaign Committee

___ Appoint Chairman of the Organizing Committee.

___ Select a secretary or note-taker.

___ Establish a schedule of committee meeting dates.

___ Set a target to date to form the Campaign Committee.

___ Review the political situation: issues, opposition, community attitudes, name recognition, support bases.

___ Gather information on filing dates and requirements.

___ Get the FPPC Manual and forms.

___ Gather costs for printing, mailing, advertising.

___ Check voting patterns in recent elections.

___ List supporters, contributors, volunteers.

___ Draft preliminary budget.

___ Plan and begin fundraising.

___ Open bank account.

___ Print Candidate Fact Sheet.

___ Print Pledge/Endorsement/Volunteer cards.

___ Decide general campaign strategy.

___ Decide campaign organization.

___ List campaign materials in priority order.

___ Set tentative date to announce candidacy; plan event.

___ Form the Campaign Committee.

CAMPAIGN COMMITTEE

Titles and Job Descriptions

(This is a comprehensive list of titles and functions to aid you in forming a Campaign Committee to meet your needs.)

Campaign Manager: Runs the show; chairs Steering Committee; only person who can authorize spending money.

Campaign Chairman: A "name" person to attract support; may also manage campaign; sometimes an honorary position.

Co-Chairmen: Honorary titles or working positions.

Honorary Chairmen: Used to attract support.

Treasurer: Required by California law; receives and banks contributions; pays all bills; keeps financial records; files Fair Political Practices Commission (FPPC) reports.

Finance Chairman: Chief fundraiser; should know community money sources and fundraising techniques.

Volunteer Chairman/Coordinator: Manages volunteers.

Precinct Chairman: Organizes volunteer activities in precincts and neighborhoods.

Steering Committee: Policy/strategy/advisory group to assist Candidate and Campaign Manager; includes Campaign Chairman, Treasurer, Finance Chairman, Volunteer or Precinct Chairman, others who know the community and campaigning.

Scheduling Chairman: Schedules Candidate's time; maintains calendar of campaign activities; sometimes runs coffee program.

continued. . .

Coffee Chairman: Organizes coffee program; finds people to host coffees in their homes; provides materials.

Publicity Chairman: Writes and places stories in news media; handles media requests and questions; may also handle advertising and speech writing.

Events Chairman: Organizes all types of events; appoints chairman for each event.

Phone Bank Chairman: Organizes Phone Banks; recruits and trains volunteers.

Get-Out-The-Vote Chairman: Organizes the election day event; recruits and trains volunteers.

Sign Committee Chairman: Oversees design and production of signs and posters; finds locations and organizes volunteers to put them up and take them down; gets signs placed in store windows and residential lawns and windows.

Endorsement Chairman: Runs endorsement program; works to secure group endorsements; maintains file of all endorsements received.

Research Director: Directs research and information-gathering activities; maintains information files.

Production Coordinator: Coordinates production of all campaign materials; establishes production schedules.

Office Manager: Directs volunteer work at permanent headquarters; often a paid position to ensure reliability.

Advertising Chairman: Designs, prepares and places paid advertising.

Speech Writer: Researches and writes speeches.

continued. . .

Special Group Chairmen: Head committees composed of people with common interests, such as business, professional, youth, retired, ethnic and other groups.

Area Chairmen: Preside over mini-campaign committees in sub-areas in campaigns covering large areas.

Precinct Captains; Block Captains: Assist the Precinct Chairman.

Budget Committee: In large campaigns, allocates funds among campaign functions.

Executive Committee: Sub-division of Steering Committee in large campaign organizations.

Advisory Committee: Sometimes formed by candidates, usually personal friends.

Campaign Secretary: Useful during organizing period to keep notes of decisions and assignments.

NOTES _____

_____

_____

_____

_____

_____

_____

_____

CAMPAIGN COMMITTEE ROSTER (p. 1)

CANDIDATE: _____ Home Ph. _____

Address: _____ Bus. Ph. _____

CAMPAIGN MGR: _____ Home Ph. _____

Address: _____ Bus. Ph. _____

CAMPAIGN CHM: _____ Home Ph. _____

Address: _____ Bus. Ph. _____

TREASURER: _____ Home Ph. _____

Address: _____ Bus. Ph. _____

FINANCE CHM: _____ Home Ph. _____

Address: _____ Bus. Ph. _____

VOL. COORD: _____ Home Ph. _____

Address: _____ Bus. Ph. _____

PRECINCT CHM: _____ Home Ph. _____

Address: _____ Bus. Ph. _____

SCHED. CHM: _____ Home Ph. _____

Address: _____ Bus. Ph. _____

COFFEE CHM: _____ Home Ph. _____

Address: _____ Bus. Ph. _____

PUBLICITY CHM: _____ Home Ph. _____

Address: _____ Bus. Ph. _____

continued. . .

CAMPAIGN COMMITTEE ROSTER

EVENTS CHM: _____ Home Ph. _____

Address: _____ Bus. Ph. _____

SIGN CHM: _____ Home Ph. _____

Address: _____ Bus. Ph. _____

ENDORSEMENTS CHM: _____ Home Ph. _____

Address: _____ Bus. Ph. _____

PHONE BANK CHM: _____ Home Ph. _____

Address: _____ Bus. Ph. _____

RESEARCH CHM: _____ Home Ph. _____

Address: _____ Bus. Ph. _____

PRODUCTION COORD: _____ Home Ph. _____

Address: _____ Bus. Ph. _____

GET-OUT-VOTE CHM: _____ Home Ph. _____

Address: _____ Bus. Ph. _____

ADVERTISING CHM: _____ Home Ph. _____

Address: _____ Bus. Ph. _____

OFFICE MGR: _____ Home Ph. _____

Address: _____ Bus. Ph. _____

NOTES _____

FILING NOMINATION PAPERS

The Candidate's Actions

Date filing period opens: _____

Deadline for filing papers: _____

Extended deadline (if any): _____

Copy of City/County Clerk Candidate Guidelines: _____

Eligible for office? _____

Ballot designation (3 words): _____

Sponsor signatures required: _____

Number obtained: _____

Checked for validity: _____

Filing fee required? _____ Cost: $_____

Number of signatures in lieu of fee: _____

Number obtained: _____ Validity checked: _____

Check in hand to pay filing fee: _____

Statement of Qualifications prepared: _____

Cost: $_____ Check in hand: _____

News release prepared: _____ Photograph: _____

Publicity event planned: _____

NOTES _____

_____

_____

_____

RESEARCH

Organizing & County Clerk Facts

ORGANIZE YOUR EFFORT:

Research Director/Coordinator: _____

List people to help: _____

Assign people to tasks; establish schedule for work.

Establish a filing system.

FACTS TO GATHER FROM COUNTY CLERK:

Filing period: Opens _____ Closes: _____

Extension deadline (if any): _____

No. sponsor signatures required: _____ Filing fee: $_____

No. voter signatures in lieu of filing fee: _____

Statement of Qualifications: Words _____ Fee $_____

Date voter list available, this election: _____

Total voters your area: _____ Voter households: _____

Cost, precinct sheets by street address: $_____

Cost, alphabetical list $_____

Cost of labels: By household $_____ By individual $_____

Other lists available: _____

Production time: Lists: _____ Labels: _____

Recall: Number of signatures required: _____

Recall: Instructions and forms: _____

RESEARCH

Printing & Advertising Costs

PRINTING: (List vendors)

Brochures, various sizes, per 1000, 5000, 10,000:

1 color _____ 2 colors _____ 3 colors _____ Flat _____
1 fold _____ 2 folds _____ With photos _____ Typesetting
and pasteup costs _____

Flyers, per 1000:

8½ x 11 _____ 8½ x 14 _____ 1 side _____ 2 sides _____
Colored paper _____ Colored ink _____ Folded _____

Letterhead, per 1000: _____ Envelopes, per 1000: _____

Rubber stamps (address), various sizes: _____

Bumper stickers, per 100: 1 color _____ 2 colors _____

Large signs, each: Painting _____ Wood _____

Lawn/window posters, per 100: 1 color _____ 2 colors _____
With stakes _____ 2 per sheet for foldover _____

Production time for each item above: _____

ADVERTISING: (List publications, broadcasters)

Page _____ ½ page _____ ¼ page _____ Per inch _____

Color(s) _____ Front page box: Size _____ Cost _____

Deadlines: _____

TV & Radio: Cost per minute, various hours _____

_____

Production facilities/costs: _____

_____

RESEARCH

Mailing--Candidates--Issues

CAMPAIGN MAILING:

Postmaster: _____ Phone: _____

Permits: Bulk mail $_____ 1st class $_____ 3rd class $_____

Rates: 1st class $_____ 3rd class $_____ Postcards $_____

Postcard sizes: Min. _____ Max. _____

3rd class delivery time: _____ Pkging/sorting: _____

Committee/printer name requirements: _____

CANDIDATE RESEARCH: (Each candidate in race.)

_____ Strengths, weaknesses, support bases.

_____ Estimate votes by precinct.

_____ Clip news items: views, positions.

_____ Voter survey: name ID, strength.

ISSUE RESEARCH:

_____ List known issues, gather material, start file.

_____ Segment of community affected by each issue.

_____ Minor "neighborhood" issues, list by neighborhood.

_____ Voter survey on issues.

_____ Rank issues according to importance, by precinct and voting group in the community.

NOTES _____

BUILDING NAME RECOGNITION

The Candidate's Actions

1. Decide whether this is a long-term or a short-term effort and plan accordingly.

2. Identify important voting "constituencies" in the community and the leadership for each one. Examples:

    * The business community.
    * Professional/occupational "communities."
    * Age, income, ethnic, church "communities."
    * Neighborhoods or areas with strong self-identity.
    * Community "shakers and movers" (influential citizens).

3. Identify constituencies where you have membership, good contact, or need to penetrate.

4. Plan strategy to penetrate important new constituencies.

5. Seek leadership opportunities in organizations in which you are a member--increase internal recognition.

6. Seek publicity opportunities--within groups, in public.

7. Be a program speaker for local groups.

8. Speak out on issues of community concern.

9. Ask friends to invite you to meetings of their groups.

10. Attend meetings of the government agency to which you want to be elected; speak out on issues.

11. Circulate in the community; participate in civic and social events.

continued. . .

12. Write letters to editors about community problems.

13. Have friends respond to your letters, supporting your views.

14. Conduct your own "surveys" on topics of community interest, walking neighborhoods with a clipboard and questions.

15. Buy advertising space in the local newspaper and write your own weekly "column" about local issues.

16. Expand your Christmas card list within the community.

17. Write congratulatory notes to people you know--on appropriate occasions (anniversaries, achievements by any member of the family, etc.).

18. Maintain a card file of people you know and meet; list pertinent information, such as groups they belong to, interests you have in common, their interests in local politics their potential value in a campaign.

19. Make lists of people who express interest in helping you to get elected--as volunteers or contributors.

20. Involve a few good friends in the recognition project.

NOTES _____

_____

_____

_____

_____

_____

_____

CAMPAIGN PLAN

ORGANIZE TO PLAN CAMPAIGN:

____ Select planning coordinator _____

____ Form planning group.

____ Establish planning schedule.

____ Assign responsibility for each segment of the plan.

RESEARCH: (See Checklist #6)

DECIDE STRATEGIES:

____ General campaign strategy.

____ Fundraising strategy.

____ Declare candidacy: early? late?

____ Handling announcement: reception? news conference?

____ Issues: priorities, positions, how to handle.

____ Opposition candidates: how to handle.

____ Publicity and advertising.

____ Endorsements.

____ Phone Bank and Get-Out-The-Vote campaign.

____ Signs and posters: type, number, style, location.

____ Speeches and debates.

ALLIES AND OPPOSITION:

____ List by type, interest, size, strength, importance.

____ Identify leadership among allies and opposition groups.

____ Identify strongest allies; decide how to use them.

____ Identify major opposition groups; decide strategy.

continued. . .

PROGRAM AND ACTIVITIES:

____ List options available.

____ Decide which appropriate for your campaign.

____ Make final list, in priority order.

CAMPAIGN MATERIALS:

____ Review Checklist #11; select materials to use.

____ Get costs, production time, production requirements.

____ Make priority list.

____ Establish production schedule.

CAMPAIGN ORGANIZATION:

____ Review Checklist #3; decide combinations of functions.

____ Use Checklist #4 for organization roster.

BUDGET:

____ Draft minimum and maximum budgets.

TIMETABLE:

____ Write schedule of preparations and actions.

REVIEW AND UPDATE:

____ Review/approval by Steering Committee.

____ Set schedule for periodic review and revision of the plan.

NOTES _____

_____

_____

_____

JOBS FOR VOLUNTEERS

GENERAL

___ Answer phones

___ Make calls

___ Type

___ File

___ Drive car

___ Errands

___ Gather information

___ Organize information

___ Gather information: filing to run; mailing, advertising, printing, other costs.

___ Research: issues, candidates, voting patterns.

___ Order: voting lists, labels, precinct maps.

___ Assemble lists: contributors, supporters.

___ Make card files.

___ Set up files.

___ Recruit volunteers.

___ Fundraising.

DURING THE CAMPAIGN

___ Phoning

___ Duplicate materials

___ Distribute materials

___ Maintain calendars

___ Bulletin board

___ Scrapbook

___ Take pictures

___ Find sign sites

___ Get owners' permission

___ Put up signs/posters

___ Paint signs

___ Maintain lists/files

___ Organize events

___ Work on events

___ Phone bank/polls/surveys

___ Get-out-the-vote

___ Host a coffee/reception

___ Precinct work

___ Clip newspapers

___ Recruit volunteers

___ Fundraising

FUNDRAISING

Planning, Organizing, Preparation

Finance Chairman: _____

Treasurer: _____

PRELIMINARY ACTIONS:

____ Recruit committee members.

____ Open bank account (two signatures).

____ Set up financial record system.

____ Treasurer: File for Idenification Number with California Secretary of State--immediately, or when $500 has been collected or spent by Campaign Committee.

____ Campaign budget: Max. $_____ Min. $_____

____ Start-up amt. needed $_____ Date _____

____ Other key dates money need _____

STRATEGY CONSIDERATIONS:

____ Major or minor effort with individual contributors?

____ Major or minor effort with organizations, PACs, etc.?

____ How much emphasis on fundraising events?

____ Dollar limit on organization contributions?

____ How early to start.

____ Which appeals to use: individuals, organizations.

____ Use direct mail appeal? Which groups?

continued. . .

CONTRIBUTOR LISTS:

____ Major donors: individual, organization.

____ Individuals.

____ Organizations: companies, associations, PACs.

____ In-kind services: printing, signs, other.

FUNDRAISING MATERIALS:

____ Candidate Fact Sheet (interim use).

____ Candidate brochure.

____ Pledge/Endorsement/Volunteer cards.

____ Interim pledge cards (Xerox or other sheets).

____ Campaign stationery and envelopes.

____ Pledge envelopes.

____ Rubber stamp for committee name/address.

____ Letters to potential contributors.

____ Direct mail materials.

FUNDRAISING ACTIVITIES LIST:

____ Invitational events: receptions, luncheons, dinners.

____ Auctions, door prizes, dances, garage sales, other.

____ Personal contacts: Candidate, committee members.

____ Outside hosts for events.

OTHER:

____ Calendar of fundraising activities/events.

____ Fundraising budget: $_____

____ FPPC reports (filed by Treasurer).

CAMPAIGN MATERIALS

PRIORITY ITEMS

___ Campaign plan
___ Budget
___ Candidate Fact Sheet
___ Pledge/Endorsement/
     Volunteer cards
___ Nomination papers
___ Qualifications statement
___ Petition in lieu of
     filing fee
___ Lists: supporters,
     contributors, volunteers
___ Bank account
___ News releases
___ Photograph (face)
___ Scheduling calendar

ADMINISTRATIVE MATERIALS

___ Checklists
___ FPPC Manual & forms
___ Financial records
___ Voter lists/labels/maps
___ Postal information
___ Sign ordinances/fees
___ Letterhead/envelopes
___ Sign-in sheets
___ Newspaper clippings
___ Scrapbook

BASIC CAMPAIGNING MATERIALS

___ Brochure(s)
___ Fact sheets
___ Flyers/leaflets
___ Signs and posters
___ "Dear Friend" cards
___ Invitations for events
___ News releases
___ Advertisements
___ Phone Bank materials
___ Thank you letters

OPTIONAL ADDITIONAL MATERIALS

___ Bumper stickers
___ Position papers
___ Newsletters
___ Target group mailings
___ Advertising inserts
___ Ad/Editorial reprints
___ Cartoons
___ Door hangers
___ Novelty items
___ Balloons
___ Video tapes
___ Audio tapes
___ Slide shows
___ Motion pictures

NOTES _____

INVITATIONAL EVENTS
(Receptions, Fundraisers, Luncheons, Dinners)

Basic Planning Decisions

PURPOSE:
___ Fundraising
___ Publicity
___ Other: _____

AUDIENCE:
___ Contributors
___ Public
___ Target group
___ Other: _____

TIMING:
___ Weekday
___ Weekend
___ Midday
___ Afternoon
___ Evening

LOCATION:
___ Indoors
___ Outdoors
___ Private
___ Rented

DRESS:
___ Formal
___ Informal
___ Costume

INVITATIONS:
___ RSVP
___ No RSVP
___ Mail
___ Phone
___ Publicity/Adv.

BUDGET: $_____

FOOD & SERVICE:
___ Snacks
___ Buffet
___ Sit-down meal
___ Other: _____
___ Catered
___ Volunteers

BEVERAGES:
___ Open bar
___ No host bar
___ Champagne
___ Wine
___ Beer
___ Whiskey/Gin, etc.
___ Punch (alcoholic)
___ Punch (plain)
___ Soft drinks
___ Coffee/tea

PROGRAM:
___ Live music
___ Records/Tape
___ Entertainment
___ Guest speaker
___ VIP introductions
___ Master of Ceremonies

FINANCING:
___ Ticket sales
___ Campaign budget
___ Outside host/sponsor

CHAIRMAN: _____

INVITATIONAL EVENTS

Invitations Committee

(Use after type and nature of event is decided.)

____ Assemble lists:
(Include name, spouse's name, home address, phone.)

    ____ VIPs and special guests.

    ____ Elected officials and civic leaders.

    ____ Editors, publishers and broadcast executives.

    ____ Campaign Committee and volunteers.

____ Establish printing and mailing schedule.

____ Design invitations:

    ____ Time, place and date of event.

    ____ Purpose of event.

    ____ Dress.

    ____ Cost, if any.

    ____ RSVP instructions.

____ Print invitations.

____ Address and mail invitations.

____ Record RSVP responses.

____ Follow-up calls.

____ VIP list to Publicity Chairman.

____ Acceptance list to: Candidate, Campaign Manager, Event Chairman, Hospitality Committee, Publicity Chairman.

INVITATIONAL EVENTS

Facility & Decorations Committee

(Use after type and nature of event is decided.)

____ Recruit volunteers for committee.

____ Select site and negotiate agreement.

____ Obtain key to building and/or room.

____ Check for:

    ____ Refrigerator.

    ____ Stove.

    ____ Pots, pans, cooking utensils.

    ____ Dishwashing facilities.

    ____ Restrooms (with paper and towels).

____ Locate light, heat, air conditioning controls.

____ Arrange for emergency service: elec., heat, air cond.

____ Determine need for chairs, tables, other items.

____ Decide decorations theme: walls, tables, head table.

____ Make or contract for decorations.

____ Decorations for Hospitality Committee table.

____ Decorations list:

    ____ Banners.   ____ Place cards.

    ____ Pictures.   ____ American flag/base.

    ____ Bunting.   ____ California flag/base.

    ____ Balloons.   ____ Table cloths.

    ____ Flowers.

INVITATIONAL EVENTS

Food & Beverage Committee Checklist

(Use after type and nature of event is decided.)

GENERAL PLANNING:

___ Menu (snacks/meal)

___ Caterer arrangements.

___ Volunteers catering.

___ Food purchase/storage.

___ Food servers.

___ Surplus food disposal.

___ Garbage/trash disposal.

___ Bar/beverage list.

___ Purchase and storage.

___ Surplus disposal plan.

___ Bar open/close times.

___ Bar ticket sales.

___ Meal ticket collection.

BAR SERVICE EQUIPMENT:

___ Bar tools.

___ Glasses.

___ Napkins

___ Bar towels.

___ Trash bag.

MEAL PREPARATION EQUIPMENT:

___ Refrigerator.

___ Storage area.

___ Stove.

___ Pots and pans.

___ Cooking utensils.

___ Hotpads.

___ Condiments/spices.

___ Serving dishes.

___ Garbage can/bags.

___ Trash bags.

___ Washing facilities.

___ Soap/towels.

___ Paper towels.

MEAL SERVICE SUPPLIES:

___ Plates, cups, saucers.

___ Knives, forks, spoons.

___ Napkins.

___ Salt & pepper shakers.

___ Condiments

INVITATIONAL EVENTS

Program Committee Checklist

(Use after type and nature of event is decided.)

____ Background music during cocktail hour.

____ Music during meal/reception.

____ Schedule: entertainment, speaker(s), presentations.

____ Public address system.

____ Projector and screen.

____ Podium, with light.

____ Contracts/agreements with entertainers/speaker(s).

____ Special needs of entertainers/speaker(s).

____ Locate light controls; fuse boxes.

____ Provide information for m.c. to introduce people.

____ Assign people to meet entertainers/speaker(s).

____ Coordinate: Event Chairman, Publicity, Master of Ceremonies, Campaign Manager, Candidate.

____ Treasurer pay for entertainers/speaker(s).

____ Candidate sign thank you letters.

____ Return borrowed equipment.

NOTES _____

_____

_____

INVITATIONAL EVENTS

Publicity Checklist

(Use after type and nature of event is decided.)

____ Plan publicity/advertising program and schedule: news releases, ads, flyers, posters, etc.

____ Media list, including deadlines and contacts.

____ Name lists for publicity: VIPs, special guests, entertainers, speaker(s), volunteer organizers.

____ Initial news release announcing event: date, time, place, purpose, VIPs, program, volunteer organizers.

____ Additional news releases.

____ Invite media with Memo to Editors: date, time, place, purpose, VIPs, program, time Candidate or speaker(s) will talk.

____ Ask editors if they want followup stories/pictures.

____ Provide followup stories/pictures for media not present.

____ Call reporters the day before the event--reminder.

____ Assign people to greet and assist reporters/photographers.

____ Plan photo coverage for campaign use: color, B&W.

____ Coordinate plans with Event Chairman, Campaign Manager, Candidate, Master of Ceremonies.

NOTES _____

_____

_____

_____

INVITATIONAL EVENTS

Finance Committee Checklist

(Use after type and nature of event is decided.)

____ Budget for the event: $ _____

____ Funding sources:

    ____ Ticket sales.

    ____ Campaign budget.

    ____ Outside host.

    ____ Other: _____

____ Pledge Cards for Hospitality Committee table.

____ Bowls, boxes, other receptacles for contributions.

____ Tickets and sales program.

____ Gifts, prizes, other fundraising items.

____ Arrange time in program to ask for contributions.

____ Arrange for first few contributions to get the action started.

____ Read FPPC rules regarding cash contributions.

____ Pick up and tabulate contributions; safeguard them.

____ Turn over all contributions to Treasurer.

____ Coordinate plans: Event Chairman, Campaign Manager, Treasurer, Candidate.

____ Have Candidate sign thank you letters to contributors.

NOTES _____

_____

INVITATIONAL EVENTS

Hospitality Committee Checklist

(Use after type and nature of event is decided.)

PREPARATIONS:

___ Recruit volunteers.

___ Table for sign-in book and campaign materials.

___ Chairs for Hospitality volunteers.

___ Sign-in book or sheets: space for names, addresses and telephone numbers of guests.

___ Name tags for Hospitality Committee. (Make in advance)

___ Name tags for guests. (Make in advance if possible.)

___ Spare name tags.

___ Ball point pens for sign-in.

___ Felt pens for name tags.

___ Pins to attach name tags.

___ Campaign materials on hand (pledge cards, brochures, etc.).

AT EVENTS:

___ Greet each incoming guest.

___ Ask guests to sign in.

___ Provide name tags.

___ Introduce guests to Candidate and others.

___ Give sign-in book/sheets to Campaign Manager.

___ Give surplus campaign materials to Campaign Manager.

___ Give extra name tags and pens to Campaign Manager.

INVITATIONAL EVENTS

Master of Ceremonies Checklist

(Use after type and nature of event is decided.)

____ Timetable of events.

____ List of people to introduce.

____ Check list against sign-in sheet.

____ Notes for introducing Candidate.

____ Notes for introducing entertainers/speaker(s).

____ Seating plan to introduce head table.

____ Coordinate plans: Event Chairman, Campaign Manager, Candidate, speaker(s).

NOTES _____

_____

_____

_____

_____

_____

_____

_____

_____

_____

INVITATIONAL EVENTS

Clean-up Committee Checklist

(Use after type and nature of event is decided.)

NOTE: Your job begins immediately after the event ends. Don't hesitate to ask for volunteers during the event.

____ Large plastic leaf bags for paper/other dry trash.

____ Plastic bags for wet garbage.

____ Boxes for utensils, bottles, equipment.

____ Separate boxes/bags for items to be washed.

____ Brooms, dust pans, cleaning cloths.

____ Soap and towels for washing utensils/equipment.

____ Names of owners of borrowed items.

____ Instructions for disposing of surplus food/beverages.

____ Gather left-over campaign materials and lost personal items; give to Campaign Manager or Event Chairman.

____ Remove table and wall decorations; give to Event Chairman.

____ Stack chairs; clean tables.

____ Sweep room; turn lights off.

____ Return key to room to Event Chairman.

NOTES _____

_____

_____

_____

NEWS RELEASES

Format & Contents

___ Topic and release date approved by Campaign Manager.

___ Distribution list prepared.

___ Envelopes addressed to media.

___ Number of copies needed: Media _____ Other _____

___ Delivery method: By hand _____ By mail _____

___ Heading includes:

   ___ Committee name and address.

   ___ Contact person, with phone number.

   ___ Date release given to media.

   ___ News release number.

___ Release typed, double-spaced, one side of paper.

___ Lead (first) paragraph:

   ___ First sentence gets reader's attention.

   ___ Answers: Who, What, When, Where, How, Why.

___ Facts presented in order of importance.

___ Opinions attributed to people by name.

___ Quotes used to improve readability and for emphasis.

___ Accuracy check: names, places, facts, dates, numbers.

___ Attachments indicated at end of story--and enclosed.

___ Photos captioned, including committee name/address.

NOTES _____

ADVERTISEMENTS

PUBLICATION NAME: _____

AD CONTACT PERSON: _____

Ad size: _____ Cost: $ _____

Publication date(s): _____

Deadline(s): _____

Proofread date: _____ Final corrections: _____

PREPARING ADVERTISEMENTS:

___ Layout prepared for the publication.

___ Type faces and sizes indicated on layout.

___ Photos marked for size and screen.

___ Committee name, address, Chairman or Treasurer included.

___ Committee Identification Number included.

___ Committee type size per FPPC requirements.

___ Accuracy checked: names, places, dates, spelling, numbers.

___ Insertion order written; delivered with layout and copy.

___ Payment included with insertion order.

OTHER:

___ Proofread for typographic errors.

___ Proofread for appearance and clarity.

___ Copies for files and other uses.

___ Reprints desired? Number _____

COFFEES

Chairman, Hostess, Candidate Responsibilities

COFFEE CHAIRMAN:

___ Find hostesses; set coffee dates and times.

___ Give hostess instructions and assistance.

___ Deliver materials day before each coffee:

Brochures ___ Pledge cards ___ Notes to introduce
Candidate ___ Sign-in sheet ___ Blank name tags ___
Felt/ball point pens ___

___ Give Candidate hostess name, address, arrival time, information on hostess and guests.

___ Pick up surplus materials the day after each coffee.

___ Maintain calendar of coffees scheduled.

HOSTESS

___ Select coffee date and time; invite guests.

___ Refreshments.

___ Table for campaign materials and sign-in sheet.

___ Make name tags; ask guests to sign in.

___ Introduce Candidate to start proceedings.

CANDIDATE:

___ Arrive on time! Meet each guest.

___ Brief presentation; leave ample time for questions.

___ Pick up sign-in sheet; give to Coffee Chairman.

___ Make note of people offering to work or contribute.

___ Write thank you note to hostess.

"DEAR FRIEND" CARDS

____ Design card: Print one side: _____ two sides: _____

____ Mailing: First class: ____ Third class: _____

____ Postage: Campaign pays: _____ Sender pays: _____

____ Write message.

____ Decide number to print.

____ Order cards printed.

____ List of names of people to sign cards.

____ Instructions for people signing cards.

____ Batch cards in packages of 25, with instructions.

____ Establish control sheet.

____ Give out cards to be signed and returned to committee.

____ Followup calls to get all cards returned.

____ Mail cards about 5 days before election (if First Class), or 8-10 days before election (if Third Class).

NOTES _____

_____

_____

_____

_____

_____

_____

_____

_____

SIGNS & POSTERS

(NOTE: Signs are large, usually hand-painted on wood. Posters are printed in various sizes on heavy paper, used in windows, on lawns, along roadways or nailed on posts and fences.)

PREPARATION:

___ Obtain city and county sign ordinances from Public Works depts.

___ Select color theme.

___ Design signs/posters.

___ Check production costs.

___ Look for volunteer labor and materials.

___ Look for in-kind contribution for production.

___ Select sign sites along major roadways.

___ Select poster sites.

___ Ask business owners to put posters in windows.

___ Recruit homeowners for window/lawn posters.

___ Pay fee or deposit requited by city/county.

___ Volunteers to put up & take down signs/posters.

___ Decide No. signs/posters.

___ Order/pay for production.

ACTION ITEMS:

___ Large signs up 30-45 days before election.

___ Additional signs up in last 20 days.

___ Posters: observe community customs on time to put up.

___ Save about 1/3 of posters for last 10 days of campaign.

___ **Avoid** putting signs on utility company poles.

___ Get owners' written permission for signs/posters on private property.

___ Follow city/county rules on roadway signs/posters.

___ Replace damaged posters.

___ Remove all signs/posters immediately after election.

___ Reclaim city/county deposits; return to Treasurer.

PHONE BANKS

(NOTE: Voter registration closes 30 days before each election. Then it takes time for County Clerks to revise lists and up to two weeks for printouts, plus your time to add missing phone numbers. Thus, it's best to use voter lists available when candidates file nomination papers.)

PREPARATION:

___ Select chairman at least 6 weeks before election.

___ Order precinct sheets, by street address, 6 weeks before election.

___ Volunteers to update precinct sheets.

___ Volunteers to make calls.

___ Add missing phone numbers.

___ List precincts in priority order, per size & voter turnout.

___ Write instructions and script for callers.

___ Find calling sites.

___ Select days/times for calls to voters.

___ Provide rulers, pencils, "highlight" felt pens.

___ Store marked precinct sheets in a safe place.

RUNNING PHONE BANKS:

___ Make calls 6-8:30 p.m., Mon. through Thu.

___ Assign callers to sites.

___ Assign supervisors.

___ Issue precinct sheets, instructions, script, rulers, pencils, pens.

___ Call households only; talk to any registered voter.

___ Record responses: S - support; O - opposed; U -undecided; X - unaware of election or candidate.

___ Line out wrong/disconnected numbers.

___ Call back busy lines and no answers.

___ Note names offering to work in campaign.

___ Note names asking for more information.

___ Allow 5 rings before hanging up no-answer calls.

ELECTION DAY "GET-OUT-THE-VOTE" CAMPAIGN

ADVANCE PREPARATIONS:

___ Phone Bank (3-5 weeks before election) See Checklist #18.

___ Marked Phone Bank precinct sheets (for telephoners).

___ Precinct sheets by street address (for poll-watchers).

___ Instructions for poll-watchers.

___ Instructions for telephoners.

___ Instructions for drivers.

___ Maps for drivers.

___ Polling place addresses for poll-watchers and drivers.

___ Headquarters site and incoming phone line.

___ Phone sites: outgoing lines for telephoners.

___ Volunteers: poll-watchers, telephoners, drivers.

___ Assignment sheet: master list, volunteers/duties.

___ Supplies: pencils, rulers, erasers.

ELECTION DAY:

___ Materials precinct sheets, instructions, supplies.

___ Volunteers assemble 4 p.m.--dispatch to work sites.

___ Check polls, beginning 4:30 p.m.; again 6:30 p.m.

___ Call supporters who have not voted, starting 5:00 p.m.

___ Stop calling at 7:30 p.m.

___ Adjourn to Victory Party.

NOTES _____

POLLS & SURVEYS

Planning Decisions

PURPOSE OF THE POLL:

___ Candidate name recognition.

___ Support/opposition.

___ Ranking all candidates.

___ Issue identification.

___ Issue importance.

___ Other: _____

INFORMATION NEEDED:

___ Age.

___ Sex.

___ Education.

___ Ethnic group.

___ Religion.

___ Income level.

___ Occupation/profession.

___ Time in community.

___ Homeowner.

___ Renter.

___ Marital status.

___ Time in community.

___ Other: _____

SURVEY METHOD TO USE:

___ Telephone interview.

___ Personal interview.

___ Random sampling voters.

___ Target group/area.

___ Community leaders only.

___ Random calls.

___ Open/closed questions.

TIME TO MAKE SURVEY:

___ Time before election____

___ Time of day: _____

___ Days of week: _____

___ Total days/hours: _____

___ Time per interview: ____

DISTRIBUTION & USE OF RESULTS:

___ Steering Commiteee.

___ Full Campaign Committee.

___ News media.

___ Planning purposes only.

___ For campaign materials.

___ Other: _____

POLLS & SURVEYS

Preparation & Action Checklist

(NOTE: This list is for attitude/opinion surveys. For candidate recognition/ranking, limit questions to that topic.

PREPARATIONS:

___ Voter lists.

___ Update phone numbers.

___ Draft questions.

___ Field test for clarity and lack of bias.

___ Rewrite questions.

___ Organize sequence: issues/problems first; demographics last.

___ Decide sample size: i.e. 10%, every 10th name.

___ Select phone sites.

___ Tally system.

___ Questions, instructions, script for callers.

___ Caller work schedule.

___ Rulers, pencils, erasers.

___ Recruit, train volunteers.

___ Designate supervisors.

CONDUCTING POLL/SURVEY

___ Make calls 6-8:30 p.m., Mon. through Thu.

___ Assign callers to sites.

___ Assign supervisors.

___ Issue precinct sheets, questions, instructions, script, equipment.

___ Ask for voters by name on precinct sheets.

___ OK to talk to spouse, if registered voter.

___ No phone or disconnected, go to next name on list.

___ Allow 5 rings before hanging up.

___ Surveys: as questions as worded, in sequence. No deviations!

___ Polls: rotate sequence of candidate names.

___ Completed all sheets before re-calling busy lines or no answers.

___ Tally results.

CAMPAIGN HEADQUARTERS

Equipment & Supplies

EQUIPMENT

___ Office space
___ Keys to office
___ Telephone
___ Desks
___ Tables
___ Chairs
___ File cabinet (locking)
___ Typewriters
___ Typewriter stands
___ Phone books
___ Bulletin board
___ Blackboard
___ Precinct maps
___ Staplers
___ 3-hole punch
___ Rolodex file
___ 3x5 card file boxes
___ Petty cash box (locking)
___ Waste baskets
___ Copy machine available
___ Scissors
___ Rulers
___ Hot plate
___ Coffee pot
___ Broom
___ Dust pan
___ Refrigerator
___ Pencil sharpener
___ Picnic cooler
___ Reverse Directory

SUPPLIES

___ Letterhead stationery
___ Envelopes (letter)
___ Envelopes (large)
___ Typing paper
___ Carbon paper
___ White-out
___ Scratch paper
___ Note/message pads
___ Clip boards
___ 3-ring binders
___ File folders/labels
___ Tabbed dividers
___ Pencils (with erasers)
___ Ball point pens
___ Felt pens (several colors)
___ Chalk
___ Thumb tacks/map pins
___ 3x5 cards (plain)
___ 3x5 cards (lined)
___ Calendars: wall/desk
___ Rubber stamp (campaign name & address)
___ Ink pad
___ Paper plates/cups
___ Styrofoam cups
___ Plastic utensils
___ Plastic trash bags
___ Coffee, tea
___ Sugar, cream

CAMPAIGN HEADQUARTERS

Staff & Materials

STAFF

___ Office manager

___ Receptionists

___ Telephone receptionist

___ Volunteers

___ Program coordinators

___ Publicity workers

WORKING MATERIALS

___ Lists:

    ___ Campaign workers

    ___ Contributors

    ___ Supporters

    ___ Media news

    ___ News reporters

___ Work schedules (posted)

___ Events calendar

___ Speaking Calendar

___ Campaign fact book

___ News clips (posted)

___ Petty cash fund

___ Postage stamps

CAMPAIGN MATERIALS

___ Brochure(s)

___ Pledge cards

___ Fact sheets

___ Signs and posters

___ "Dear Friend" cards

___ Bumper stickers

___ Door hangers

___ News releases

___ Editorial reprints

___ Ad reprints

___ Newsletters

___ Buttons

___ Giveaway items

___ Newsletters

___ Position papers

___ Flyers

___ Leaflets

___ Cartoons

___ Pictures

___ Other materials: _____

_____